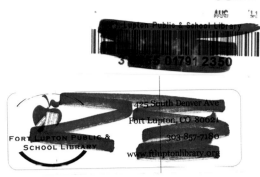

AMERICAN LITERATURE FROM 1945 THROUGH TODAY

THE BRITANNICA GUIDE TO WORLD LITERATURE

AMERICAN
LITERATURE
FROM 1945 THROUGH TODAY

EDITED BY ADAM AUGUSTYN,
ASSISTANT MANAGER AND ASSISTANT EDITOR, LITERATURE

Britannica®
Educational Publishing

IN ASSOCIATION WITH

ROSEN
EDUCATIONAL SERVICES

Published in 2011 by Britannica Educational Publishing
(a trademark of Encyclopædia Britannica, Inc.)
in association with Rosen Educational Services, LLC
29 East 21st Street, New York, NY 10010.

Distributed exclusively by Rosen Educational Services.
For a listing of additional Britannica Educational Publishing titles, call toll free (800) 237-9932.

First Edition

Britannica Educational Publishing
Michael I. Levy: Executive Editor
J.E. Luebering: Senior Manager
Marilyn L. Barton: Senior Coordinator, Production Control
Steven Bosco: Director, Editorial Technologies
Lisa S. Braucher: Senior Producer and Data Editor
Yvette Charboneau: Senior Copy Editor
Kathy Nakamura: Manager, Media Acquisition
Adam Augustyn: Assistant Manager and Assistant Editor, Literature

Rosen Educational Services
Jeanne Nagle: Senior Editor
Heather M. Moore Niver: Editor
Nelson Sá: Art Director
Cindy Reiman: Photography Manager
Matthew Cauli: Designer, Cover Designer
Introduction by Greg Roza

Library of Congress Cataloging-in-Publication Data

American literature from 1945 through today / edited by Adam Augustyn. — 1st ed.
    p. cm. — (The Britannica guide to world literature)
"In association with Britannica Educational Publishing, Rosen Educational Services."
Includes bibliographical references and index.
ISBN 978-1-61530-133-1 (library binding)
1. American literature--20th century—History and criticism. 2. American literature—
21st century—History and criticism. 3. American literature—20th
century—Bio-bibliography. 4. American literature—21st century—Bio-bibliography. 5.
Authors, American—20th century—Biography. 6. Authors, American—21st century—
Biography. I. Augustyn, Adam, 1979-
PS225.A44 2011
810.9'0054--dc22

2010002166

Manufactured in the United States of America

On the cover: Toni Morrison (left) and Jack Kerouac are part of a bounty of postwar
American literary masters that span a larger range of heritages and backgrounds than ever
before. *James Keyser/Time & Life Pictures/Getty Images (Morrison); Hulton Archive/Getty Images
(Kerouac).*

CONTENTS

31

38

52

64

86

88

122

126

143

151

158

177

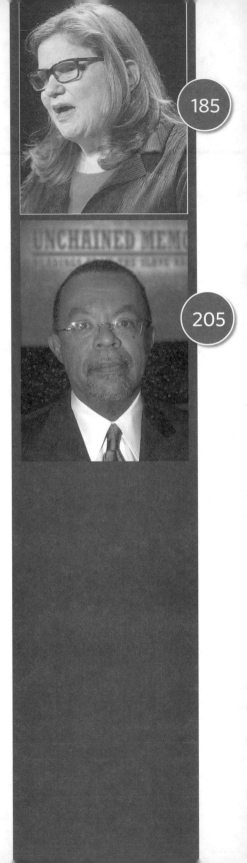

185

205

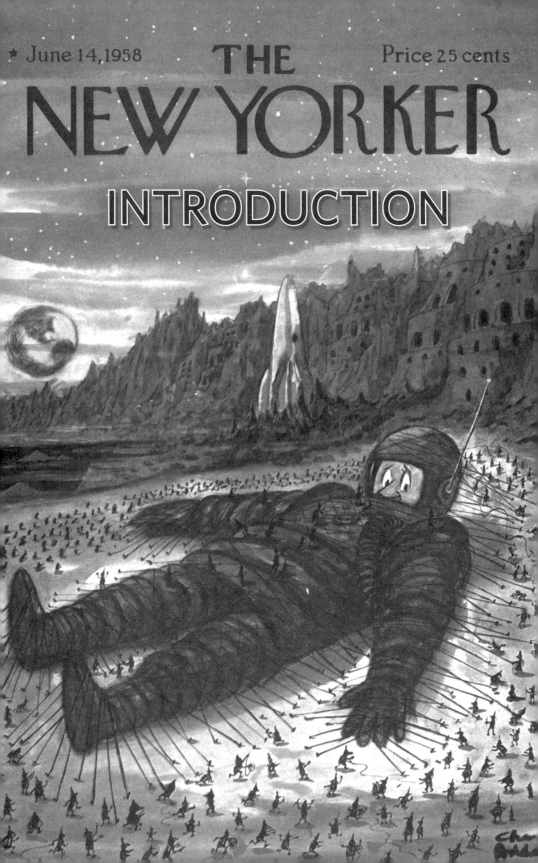

In the words of literary historian Malcolm Cowley, the literature that emerged in the United States in the time between the two world wars represented a "second flowering" of American literature. Novelists such as William Faulkner and Ernest Hemingway, dramatists such as Eugene O'Neill, and poets such as Marianne Moore and Robert Frost represented a transformation in form and style. The daring writers of that era had a lasting influence on the postwar writers who followed in their footsteps.

Two groups of American writers responded with distinct approaches to the events of World War II. The first approached the subject matter by way of realism, as best seen in the writings of Norman Mailer. Mailer was one of the founders of the new journalism movement, which combined subjective literary qualities with an objective journalistic style. His fiction and nonfiction writings attacked the totalitarianism that he had come to believe was intrinsically linked with U.S. politics.

While writers like Mailer, Irwin Shaw, and James Jones employed realism to depict World War II, others used satire and black humour. Drawing on his war experiences to create a farcical look at the military mindset, Joseph Heller's *Catch-22* (1961) became one of the era's pre-eminent protest novels. Kurt Vonnegut published *Slaughterhouse-Five* (1969), a satirical novel centred on his harrowing experiences as a U.S. prisoner of war in Dresden, Ger. The book also features wild digressions from the very real horrors of World War II into time travel and alien abduction, which link the work and Vonnegut himself with a new movement in postwar American literature: absurdism.

June 14, 1958, cover of The New Yorker. *Since 1925, this periodical has been a vibrant forum for several notable American short story writers, novelists, essayists, and poets.* Apic//Hulton Archive/Getty Images

Absurdism marked a distinct shift away from realism. Writers of the absurdist movement used startlingly creative techniques to express deeply personal emotions in new ways. Absurdist plots often centre around fantastic events, and many absurdist novels openly address their very existence as pieces of literature, a technique that allows them to be classed as metafiction.

One of the finest early practitioners of absurdism was the Russian-born novelist Vladimir Nabokov. After he moved to the United States, he wrote the groundbreaking and controversial novel *Lolita* (1955). Considered by many the greatest American novel of the 20th century, *Lolita* is known for its rich language and innovative style. Other notable American authors in the absurdist movement include John Barth, Thomas Pynchon, and William S. Burroughs.

Despite the experimentation of the absurdists, social realism was still a major force in American literature through the second half of the 20th century. Many authors sought to describe postwar America through intensely personal explorations. Saul Bellow's novel *The Adventures of Augie March* (1953) follows an impoverished Chicago boy as he navigates the course of America after the Great Depression. Novelist Philip Roth shed light on middle-class American Jewish society in novels some considered offensive; but his portrayals of race, sexuality, love, and mortality are profound. John Updike is renowned for his stories of middle-class American life. One of his best novels, *Rabbit, Run* (1960), tells the story of a small-town family man and former star high school athlete who flees responsibility. Updike's series of Rabbit books (*Rabbit, Run* was followed by three sequels) explore themes such as uncertainty, discontentment, sexual and moral confusion, and death.

Southern writers at this time followed the rich traditions started by William Faulkner earlier in the century. Notables among this group were several important female voices, including Flannery O'Connor, Eudora Welty, and Carson McCullers. O'Connor's darkly comic explorations of the grotesque have aged particularly well, and she has come to be regarded as one of the preeminent writers of the century, despite her modest output—only two novels and a number of short stories.

In 1965 southern writer Truman Capote published *In Cold Blood*. After hearing of a mass murder in Kansas, Capote spent more than five years interviewing people connected to the case. He used thousands of pages of notes to create a work of nonfiction that used elements of fiction, particularly suspense and vivid descriptions of events. Experts have criticized Capote for fabricating details and dialogue in the book, but many consider it the forerunner of the true crime genre.

After World War II African American authors moved away from the traditions of the Harlem Renaissance. Writers such as James Baldwin and Ralph Ellison sought to portray fully the complexities and difficulties of life for African Americans. Ellison's *The Invisible Man* (1952) is told by an African American man who describes what it is like to be "socially invisible" to both whites and blacks. Baldwin, Ellison, and other black writers of their era led the way for future black authors. Alice Walker received the Pulitzer Prize for her black feminist novel *The Color Purple* in 1982. Toni Morison's *Beloved* (1987) won a Pulitzer Prize in 1988, and in 1993 she became the first African American woman to receive the Nobel Prize in Literature.

Many writers endeavoured to invent new kinds of fiction to respond to the fundamental societal changes that took place in America after World War II. The post-modern movement included novelists such as William Gaddis, John Barth, John Hawkes, Donald Barthelme, Thomas Pynchon, Robert Coover, Paul Auster, and Don DeLillo, who used various experimental techniques to convey the new American reality. Many of their works are technically complex and directly address the nature of fiction and reality, often focussing on themes of paranoia, fear, and violence.

At the other end of the fictional spectrum, realist short-story writer Raymond Carver—influenced by Hemingway and the Irish writer Samuel Beckett—wrote spare yet powerfully suggestive tales. Often credited with revitalizing interest in minimalist fiction and the short story, Carver influenced many important American writers, including Richard Ford, Russell Banks, and Tobias Wolff.

American poetry was perhaps less innovative and groundbreaking than fiction in the years after World War II, but many important writers of verse rose to prominence at this time. Poets such as Theodore Roethke, Robert Lowell, Adrienne Rich, and Frank O'Hara wrote verse that has stood the test of time.

Robert Lowell and Theodore Roethke were impressive formal poets, both winning Pulitzer Prizes for their writing. Lowell's earliest poems are rife with dissonant sounds and chafing images, but his later writing eases into a more laid-back, informal style. Clearly influenced by William Butler Yeats, Roethke's writing exhibits a keen self-reflection and a heightened sensitivity toward nature. His poetry styles ranged from formal, rhyming stanzas to jovial free verse.

In the 1950s the Beat poets—led by Allen Ginsberg and spurred on by his inimitable and epic poem *Howl*—began experimenting with new styles and forms, endeavouring to free poetry from the confines of academia and bring it "back to the streets." Important Beat poets include Lawrence Ferlinghetti, Gregory Corso, Gary Snyder, and the novelist Jack Kerouac. Beat poetry performances often featured dense verse and obscenities, and some readings included progressive jazz accompaniment.

After World War II American poetry became more intensely personal and confessional, as shown in the Lowell-influenced works of Anne Sexton, Sylvia Plath, and John Berryman. Sexton's poetry garnered much attention for its vibrant imagery and unflinching honesty about her nervous breakdown and attempts at recovery. Berryman used a fair amount of humour to lighten the confessional weight of his writing, exhibiting technical flair in poetry, short stories, and even a biography of Stephen Crane. Plath is especially remembered for her poignant self-revelations, sardonic wit, and musings on life and death.

Other writers, encouraged by poet Robert Bly, moved away from the confessional styles of Sexton and Plath toward the individual voice and open forms. Bly encouraged such writers as Galway Kinnell, James Wright, and David Ignatow to seek a level of spiritual intensity rare in American poetry. The writers of this movement, such as James Dickey, are sometimes called the "deep image" poets. A former soldier and avid hunter, Dickey developed a keen insight on the topics of life and death, predator and prey, and internal versus external conflict. His volume of poems, *Buckdancer's Choice* (1965), earned him the National Book Award.

Three playwrights dominated postwar American drama: Arthur Miller, Tennessee Williams, and Edward Albee. Miller's work addressed both social concerns and inner conflict. He is best known for the Pulitzer

Prize–winning play *Death of a Salesman* (1949), an exploration of the dark side of the American dream and the struggle for success. Miller is also known for his protest writings, such as *The Crucible* (1953), which uses the theme of the Salem witch trials to protest the "witch hunts" of the McCarthy era.

Tennessee Williams often wrote exquisite short fiction, which he then adapted into plays. Williams's plays offer a tragic vision of frustrated characters on a quest for meaning in their lives. In his plays the themes of sex and violence often lie beneath a veneer of romantic idealism. His best-known plays include *A Streetcar Named Desire* (1947) and *Cat on a Hot Tin Roof* (1955), for which he won Pulitzer Prizes.

When Edward Albee emerged on the drama scene, he made a name for himself with his mastery of absurdist theatre. He started out writing poetry and a novel (never published), but he eventually penned several one-act plays. His first full-length play, *Who's Afraid of Virginia Woolf?* (1962), was undoubtedly his most successful and established him as a major voice in American theatre.

By the late 1960s and early '70s, the focus on drama in the United States shifted from Broadway to smaller, less commercially-oriented venues known as "Off-Broadway." Smaller production companies, such as the Living Theatre and the Open Theatre, garnered attention for producing innovative and daring new dramas, which mainstream Broadway theatres tended to shy away from. This trend gave voice to a whole new generation of playwrights, such as David Mamet, the playwright, director, and screenwriter who created working-class characters that spoke remarkable idiomatic dialogue. In 1979 playwright Sam Shepard won a Pulitzer Prize for *Buried Child* (1978), an Off-Broadway production. Tony Kushner, Ntozake Shange,

Wendy Wasserstein, and August Wilson also became part of the canon of leading American dramatists known for their pioneering and adventurous writing.

Just as poetry, fiction, and drama in postwar America saw growth and innovation, American literary and social critics made great strides, too. Literary criticism in the first half of the 20th century was dominated by New Criticism, which emphasized close reading of the text itself and the disregard of external texts, such as biographies. By the 1960s, however, a new era in criticism had begun. Several types of criticism gained (or re-gained) prominence, including literary biography, which focused on a writer's body of work rather than a single text. The events of World War II also led to the development of valuable social criticism, such as John Hersey's *Hiroshima* (1946). The aforementioned new journalism also had a profound effect on American literary criticism in the postwar era.

Academic critics chose to apply strict theoretical standards to their analysis of literary texts. In particular, several important American critics became supporters of the theory of deconstruction. Literary deconstruction originated in France in the 1960s, but American scholars like Paul de Man, J. Hillis Miller, and Barbara Johnson were some of its most famous adherents. Other noteworthy postwar American critics include Henry Louis Gates, Jr., bell hooks, and Edward Said. Further areas of theoretical criticism that coalesced into definitive schools of thought at this time include feminism, Marxism, and cultural criticism. Although these new methods of literary criticism certainly shed new light on many texts, they were also critiqued for their rampant use of political and ideological jargon, which was deemed generally inaccessible to the common reader.

The works produced by these academics might seem esoteric to some, but they helped pave the way for contemporary American writers reinventing American literature by opening up new ways of understanding—and appreciating—texts. The promising writers of postwar America displayed vastly different values from writers of preceding eras, representing a wider range of backgrounds, ethnicities, and viewpoints. Groups long lacking a strong voice in American society—including African Americans, Jews, feminists, and homosexuals—began to appear in and create many of the ambitious works presented in the following overview. These writers may not be as lauded as the authors of Cowley's "second flowering," but the important effect they have had, and continue to have, on American culture cannot be denied.

CHAPTER 1

NOVELS AND SHORT STORIES FROM 1945

The literary historian Malcolm Cowley described the years between the two world wars as a "second flowering" of American writing. Certainly, American literature attained a new maturity and a rich diversity in the 1920s and '30s, and significant works by several major figures from those decades were published after 1945. William Faulkner, Ernest Hemingway, John Steinbeck, and Katherine Anne Porter wrote memorable fiction, but not up to their prewar standard. Robert Frost, T.S. Eliot, Wallace Stevens, Marianne Moore, E.E. Cummings, William Carlos Williams, and Gwendolyn Brooks published important poetry. Eugene O'Neill's most distinguished play, *Long Day's Journey into Night*, appeared posthumously in 1956. Before and after World War II, Robert Penn Warren published influential fiction, poetry, and criticism. His *All the King's Men*, one of the best American political novels, won the 1947 Pulitzer Prize. Mary McCarthy became a widely read social satirist and essayist. When it first appeared in the United States in the 1960s, Henry Miller's fiction was influential primarily because of its frank exploration of sexuality. But its loose, picaresque, quasi-autobiographical form also meshed well with post-1960s fiction. With impressive new novelists, poets, and playwrights emerging after the war, there was a gradual changing of the guard.

A new generation came out of the war, and its ethnic, regional, and social character differed considerably from that of the preceding one. Among the younger writers were children of immigrants, many of them Jews; African Americans, only a few generations away from slavery; and, eventually, women, who, with the rise of feminism, were to speak in a new voice. Although the social climate of the postwar years was conservative, even conformist, some of the most hotly discussed writers were homosexuals or bisexuals, including Tennessee Williams, Truman Capote, Paul Bowles, Gore Vidal, and James Baldwin, whose dark themes and experimental methods cleared a path for Beat writers such as Allen Ginsberg, William S. Burroughs, and Jack Kerouac.

REALISM AND METAFICTION

Two distinct groups of novelists responded to the cultural effect, and especially the technological horror, of World War II. Norman Mailer's *The Naked and the Dead* (1948) and Irwin Shaw's *The Young Lions* (1948) were realistic war novels, but Mailer's book was also a novel of ideas, exploring fascist thinking and an obsession with power as elements of the military mind. James Jones, amassing a staggering quantity of closely observed detail, documented the war's human cost in an ambitious trilogy (*From Here to Eternity* [1951], *The Thin Red Line* [1962], and *Whistle* [1978]) that centred on loners who resisted adapting to military discipline. Younger novelists, profoundly shaken by the bombing of Hiroshima and the real threat of human annihilation, found the conventions of realism inadequate for treating the war's nightmarish implications. In *Catch-22* (1961), for example, Joseph Heller satirized the military mentality with surreal black comedy but also injected a sense of Kafkaesque horror.

Heller was born in 1923 in Brooklyn, N.Y. During World War II, he flew 60 combat missions as a bombardier with the U.S. Air Force in Europe. After receiving an M.A. from Columbia University in 1949, he studied at the University of Oxford (1949–50) as a Fulbright scholar. He taught English at Pennsylvania State University (1950–52) and worked as an advertising copywriter for the magazines *Time* (1952–56) and *Look* (1956–58) and as promotion manager for *McCall's* (1958–61). Meanwhile, he wrote *Catch-22* in his spare time.

Released to mixed reviews, *Catch-22* developed a cult following with its dark surrealism, and it is one of the most significant works of protest literature to appear after World War II. Centring on the antihero Captain John Yossarian, stationed at an airstrip on a Mediterranean island during World War II, the novel portrays the airman's desperate attempts to stay alive. The "catch" in *Catch-22* involves a mysterious Air Force regulation that asserts that a man is considered insane if he willingly continues to fly dangerous combat missions. If he makes the necessary formal request to be relieved of such missions, however, the very act of making the request proves that he is sane and therefore ineligible to be relieved. The term "catch-22" thereafter entered the English language as a reference to a proviso that trips one up no matter which way one turns.

Heller's later novels, including *Something Happened* (1974), an unrelievedly pessimistic novel, *Good as Gold* (1979), a satire on life in Washington, D.C., and *God Knows* (1984), a wry, contemporary-vernacular monologue in the voice of the biblical King David, were less successful. *Closing Time*, a sequel to *Catch-22*, appeared in 1994. Heller also wrote an autobiography, *Now and Then: From Coney Island to Here* (1998), and his dramatic work includes the play *We Bombed in New Haven* (1968). He died in 1999.

Other noteworthy novelists also addressed the effect of war. In *Slaughterhouse-Five* (1969), Kurt Vonnegut described

Kurt Vonnegut

(b. Nov. 11, 1922, Indianapolis, Ind. — d. April 11, 2007, New York, N.Y.)

Novelist Kurt Vonnegut is noted for his pessimistic and satirical novels that use fantasy and science fiction to highlight the horrors and ironies of 20th-century civilization.

Vonnegut studied at Cornell University before serving in the U.S. Air Force in World War II. Captured by the Germans, he was a survivor of the fire bombing of Dresden, Ger., in February 1945. After the war he studied anthropology at the University of Chicago. In the late 1940s he worked as a reporter and as a public relations writer.

Vonnegut's first novel, *Player Piano* (1952), visualizes a completely mechanized and automated society whose dehumanizing effects are unsuccessfully resisted by the scientists and workers in a New York factory town. *The Sirens of Titan* (1959) is a quasi–science fiction novel in which the entire history of the human race is considered an accident attendant on an alien planet's search for a spare part for a spaceship. In *Cat's Cradle* (1963) some Caribbean islanders adopt a new religion consisting of harmless trivialities in response to an unforeseen scientific discovery that eventually destroys all life on Earth. Vonnegut drew on his Dresden experience when writing *Slaughterhouse-Five: Or, The Children's Crusade* (1969), using that bombing raid as a symbol of the cruelty and destructiveness of war down through the centuries.

Vonnegut also wrote several plays, including *Happy Birthday, Wanda June* (1970); several works of nonfiction, such as *Wampeters, Foma & Granfalloons* (1974); and several collections of short stories, chief among which was *Welcome to the Monkey House* (1968). His other novels include *Mother Night* (1961), *God Bless You, Mr. Rosewater* (1965), *Breakfast of Champions* (1973), *Slapstick* (1976), *Jailbird* (1979), *Deadeye Dick* (1983), *Galápagos* (1985), *Bluebeard* (1987), *Hocus Pocus* (1990), and *Timequake* (1997). In 2005 he published *A Man Without a Country*, a collection of essays and speeches. Vonnegut's

Armageddon in Retrospect (2008), a collection of fiction and nonfiction that focuses on war and peace, and *Look at the Birdie* (2009), previously unpublished short stories, appeared posthumously.

the Allied firebombing of the German city of Dresden with a mixture of dark fantasy and numb, loopy humour. Later this method was applied brilliantly to the portrayal of the Vietnam War—a conflict that seemed in itself surreal—by Tim O'Brien in *Going After Cacciato* (1978) and the short story collection *The Things They Carried* (1990).

In part because of the atomic bomb, American writers increasingly turned to black humour and absurdist fantasy. Many found the naturalistic approach incapable of communicating the rapid pace and the sheer implausibility of contemporary life. A highly self-conscious fiction emerged, laying bare its own literary devices, questioning the nature of representation, and often imitating or parodying earlier fiction rather than social reality. Russian-born Vladimir Nabokov and the Argentine writer Jorge Luis Borges were strong influences on this new "metafiction." Nabokov, who became a U.S. citizen in 1945, produced a body of exquisitely wrought fiction distinguished by linguistic and formal innovation.

Nabokov was born in 1899 into an old aristocratic family in St. Petersburg, Russia. His father, V.D. Nabokov, was a leader of the pre-Revolutionary liberal Constitutional Democratic Party (Kadets) in Russia and the author of numerous books and articles on criminal law and politics, among them *The Provisional Government* (1922), which was one of the primary sources on the downfall of the Kerensky regime. In 1922, after the family had settled in Berlin, the elder Nabokov was assassinated by a reactionary rightist while shielding another man at a public meeting. Although his novelist son disclaimed any influence of this event on his art, the theme of assassination by mistake has figured prominently in Nabokov's novels. Nabokov's enormous affection for his father and the milieu in which he was raised is evident in his autobiography *Speak, Memory* (revised version, 1967).

Nabokov published two collections of verse, *Poems* (1916) and *Two Paths* (1918), before leaving Russia in 1919. He and his family made their way to England where he attended Trinity College, Cambridge, on a scholarship provided for the sons of prominent Russians in exile. While at Cambridge he first studied zoology but soon switched to French and Russian literature. He graduated with first-class honours in 1922 and subsequently wrote that his almost effortless attainment of this degree was "one of the very few 'utilitarian' sins on my conscience." While still in England he continued to write poetry, mainly in Russian but also in English, and two collections of his Russian poetry, *The Cluster* and *The Empyrean Path*, appeared in 1923. In Nabokov's mature opinion, these poems were "polished and sterile."

Between 1922 and 1940 Nabokov lived in Germany and France, and, while continuing to write poetry, he experimented with drama and even collaborated on several unproduced motion-picture scenarios. By 1925 he settled on prose as his main genre. His first short story had already been published in Berlin in 1924. His first novel, *Mashenka* (*Mary*), appeared in 1926. Avowedly autobiographical, the novel contains descriptions of the young Nabokov's first serious romance as well as of the Nabokov family estate, both of which are also described in *Speak, Memory*. Nabokov did not again draw so heavily on his personal experience as he had in *Mashenka* until his episodic novel about an émigré professor of entomology in the United States, *Pnin* (1957), which is to some extent based on his experiences while teaching (1948–58) Russian and European literature at Cornell University in Ithaca, N.Y.

His second novel, *King, Queen, Knave,* appeared in 1928, marking his turn to a highly stylized form that characterized his art thereafter. His chess novel, *The Defense,* followed two years later and won him recognition as the best of the younger Russian émigré writers. In the next five years he produced four novels and a novella. Of these, *Despair* and *Invitation to a Beheading* were his first works of importance and foreshadowed his later fame.

During his years of European emigration, Nabokov lived in a state of happy and continual semipenury. All his Russian novels were published in small editions in Berlin and Paris. His first two novels had German translations, and the money he obtained for them he used for butterfly-hunting expeditions (he eventually published 18 scientific papers on entomology). But until his best-seller *Lolita*, no book he wrote in Russian or English produced more than a few hundred dollars. During the period in which he wrote his first eight novels, he made his living in Berlin and later in Paris by giving lessons in tennis, Russian, and English and from occasional walk-on parts in films (now forgotten). His wife, the former Véra Evseyevna Slonim, whom he married in 1925, worked as a translator. From the time of the loss of his home in Russia, Nabokov's only attachment was to what he termed the "unreal estate" of memory and art. He never purchased a house, preferring instead to live in houses rented from other professors on sabbatical leave. Even after great wealth resulting from the success of *Lolita* and the subsequent interest in his previous work, Nabokov, Véra, and their son, Dmitri, lived in genteelly shabby quarters in a Swiss hotel (from 1959 until his death in 1977).

The subject matter of Nabokov's novels is principally the problem of art itself presented in various figurative

In addition to novels that were rife with allusion and wordplay, Vladimir Nabokov wrote many scientific papers on butterfly entomology. Carl Mydans/ Time & Life Pictures/Getty Images

disguises. Thus, *The Defense* seemingly is about chess, *Despair* about murder, and *Invitation to a Beheading* a political story. But all three works make statements about art that are central to understanding the book as a whole. The same may be said of his plays, *Sobytiye* (*The Event*), published in 1938, and *The Waltz Invention*. The problem of art again appears in Nabokov's best novel in Russian, *The Gift*, the story of a young artist's development in the spectral world of post–World War I Berlin. This novel, with its reliance on literary parody, was a turning point: Serious use of parody thereafter became a key device in Nabokov's art. His first novels in English, *The Real Life of Sebastian Knight* (1941) and *Bend Sinister* (1947), do not rank with his best Russian work. *Pale Fire* (1962), however, a novel consisting of a long poem and a commentary on it by a mad literary pedant, extends and completes Nabokov's mastery of unorthodox structure, first shown in *The Gift* and present also in *Solus Rex*, a Russian novel that began to appear serially in 1940 but was never completed. *Lolita* (1955), with its antihero, Humbert Humbert, who is possessed by an overpowering desire for very young girls, is yet another of Nabokov's subtle allegories: love examined in the light of its seeming opposite, lechery. *Ada* (1969), Nabokov's 17th and longest novel, is a parody of the family chronicle form. All his earlier themes come into play in the novel, and, because the work is a medley of Russian, French, and English, it is his most difficult work. (He also wrote a number of short stories and novellas, mostly written in Russian and translated into English.)

Nabokov's major critical works are an irreverent book about Nikolay Gogol (1944) and a monumental four-volume translation of, and commentary on, Pushkin's *Eugene Onegin* (1964). What he called the "present, final version" of the autobiographical *Speak, Memory*, concerning his European years, was published in 1967.

As Nabokov's reputation grew in the 1930s so did the ferocity of the attacks made upon him. His idiosyncratic, somewhat aloof style and unusual novelistic concerns were interpreted as snobbery by his detractors. However, his best Russian critic, Vladislav Khodasevich, insisted that Nabokov's aristocratic view was appropriate to his subject matters: problems of art masked by allegory.

Nabokov's reputation varies greatly from country to country. Until 1986 he was not published in the Soviet Union, not only because he was a "White Russian émigré" but also because he practiced "literary snobbism." Critics of strong social convictions in the West also generally hold him in low esteem. But within the intellectual émigré community in Paris and Berlin between 1919 and 1939, V. Sirin (the literary pseudonym used by Nabokov in those years) was credited with being "on a level with the most significant artists in contemporary European literature and occupying a place held by no one else in Russian literature." His reputation after 1940, when he changed from Russian to English after immigrating to the United States, mounted steadily until the 1970s, when he was acclaimed by a leading literary critic as "king over that battered mass society called contemporary fiction."

In an important essay, "The Literature of Exhaustion" (1967), John Barth declared himself an American disciple of Nabokov and Borges. After dismissing realism as a "used up" tradition, Barth described his own work as "novels which imitate the form of the novel, by an author who imitates the role of Author." In fact, Barth's earliest fiction, *The Floating Opera* (1956) and *The End of the Road* (1958), fell partly within the realistic tradition, but in later, more ambitious works he simultaneously imitated and parodied conventional forms. Much of Barth's writing is concerned with the seeming impossibility of choosing the right action in a world that has no absolute values.

Black Humour

Also called black comedy, black humour is writing that juxtaposes morbid or ghastly elements with comical ones that underscore the senselessness or futility of life. Black humour often uses farce and low comedy to make clear that individuals are helpless victims of fate and character.

Peter Sellers in Dr. Strangelove *(1964), directed by Stanley Kubrick.* © Columbia Pictures Corporation

Although in 1940 the French Surrealist André Breton published *Anthologie de l'humour noir* (*Anthology of Black Humour*, frequently enlarged and reprinted), the term did not come into common use until the 1960s. Then it was applied to the works of the novelists Nathanael West, Vladimir Nabokov, and Joseph Heller. The latter's *Catch-22* (1961) is a notable example, in which Captain Yossarian battles the horrors of air warfare over the Mediterranean during World War II with hilarious irrationalities matching the stupidities of the military system. Other novelists who worked in the same vein included Kurt Vonnegut, particularly in *Slaughterhouse-Five* (1969), and Thomas Pynchon, in *V* (1963) and *Gravity's Rainbow* (1973). A film exemplar is

Stanley Kubrick's *Dr. Strangelove* (1964), a comedy of militaristic errors that ends in global nuclear destruction. The term "black comedy" has been applied to playwrights in the Theatre of the Absurd, especially Eugène Ionesco, as in *Les Chaises* (produced 1952; *The Chairs*).

Antecedents to black humour include the comedies of Aristophanes (5th century BCE), François Rabelais's *Pantagruel* (1532), parts of Jonathan Swift's *Gulliver's Travels* (1726), and Voltaire's *Candide* (1759).

Barth was born in 1930, grew up on the eastern shore of Maryland—the locale of most of his writing—and studied at Johns Hopkins University in Baltimore, where he graduated with an M.A. in 1952. The next year, he began teaching at Pennsylvania State University, and in 1965 he moved to the State University of New York at Buffalo as professor of English and writer-in-residence. He was a professor of English and creative writing at Johns Hopkins University from 1973 to 1995.

Barth's first two novels, *The Floating Opera* (1956) and *The End of the Road* (1958), describe characters burdened by a sense of the futility of all action and the effects of these characters upon the less self-conscious, more active people around them. Barth forsook realism and modern settings in *The Sot-Weed Factor* (1960), a picaresque tale that burlesques the early history of Maryland and parodies the 18th-century English novel. All three novels appeared in revised editions in 1967.

Giles Goat-Boy (1966) is a bizarre tale of the career of a mythical hero and religious prophet, set in a satirical microcosm of vast, computer-run universities. His work *Lost in the Funhouse* (1968) consists of short, experimental pieces, some designed for performance, interspersed with short stories based on his own childhood. It was followed by *Chimera* (1972), a volume of three novellas, and *Letters* (1979), an experimental novel. The novels *Sabbatical* (1982) and *The Tidewater Tales* (1987) are more traditional narratives. *Once Upon a Time: A Floating Opera* (1994) combines the genres of novel and memoir in the form of a three-act opera. The novel *Coming Soon!!!* (2001) revisits *The Floating Opera* and is arguably Barth's most conspicuously self-conscious work. *The Book of Ten Nights and a Night* (2004) and *The Development* (2008) are collections of interconnected short stories.

Another author of metafiction, Donald Barthelme, mocked the fairy tale in *Snow White* (1967) and Freudian fiction in *The Dead Father* (1975). Barthelme was most successful in his short stories and parodies that solemnly caricatured contemporary styles, especially the richly suggestive pieces collected in *Unspeakable Practices, Unnatural Acts* (1968), *City Life* (1970), and *Guilty Pleasures* (1974).

The Absurdists

Thomas Pynchon emerged as the major American practitioner of the absurdist fable. His novels and stories were elaborately plotted mixtures of historical information, comic book fantasy, and countercultural suspicion that depicted human alienation in the chaos of modern society.

Pynchon was born on Long Island, N.Y., in 1937. After earning his B.A. in English from Cornell University in 1958, he spent a year in Greenwich Village writing short stories and working on a novel. In 1960 he was hired as a technical writer for Boeing Aircraft Corporation in Seattle, Wash. Two years later he decided to leave the company and write full time. In 1963 Pynchon won the Faulkner Foundation Award for his first novel, *V.* (1963), a whimsical, cynically absurd tale of a middle-aged Englishman's search for "V," an elusive, supernatural adventuress appearing in various guises at critical periods in European history. In his next book, *The Crying of Lot 49* (1966), Pynchon described a woman's strange quest to discover the mysterious, conspiratorial Tristero System in a futuristic world of closed societies. The novel serves as a condemnation of modern industrialization.

Pynchon's *Gravity's Rainbow* (1973) is a tour de force in 20th-century literature. In exploring the dilemmas of human beings in the modern world, the story, which is set in an area of post–World War II Germany called "the Zone," centres on the wanderings of an American soldier who is one of many odd characters looking for a secret V-2 rocket that will supposedly break through the Earth's gravitational barrier when launched. The narrative is filled with descriptions of obsessive and paranoid fantasies, ridiculous and grotesque imagery, and esoteric mathematical and scientific language. For his efforts Pynchon received the National Book Award, and many critics deemed *Gravity's Rainbow* a visionary, apocalyptic masterpiece. Pynchon's next novel, *Vineland*, which begins in 1984 in California, was not published until 1990. Two vast, complex historical novels followed: In *Mason & Dixon* (1997), set in the 18th century, Pynchon took the English surveyors Charles Mason and Jeremiah Dixon as his subject, whereas *Against the Day* (2006) moves from the World's Columbian Exposition of 1893 through World War I. *Inherent Vice* (2009), Pynchon's rambling take on the detective novel, returns to the California counterculture milieu of *Vineland*.

Of his few short stories, most notable are "Entropy" (1960), a neatly structured tale in which Pynchon first uses extensive technical language and scientific metaphors, and "The Secret Integration" (1964), a story in which Pynchon explores small-town bigotry and racism. The collection *Slow Learner* (1984) contains "The Secret Integration." Pynchon's technique would later influence writers as different as Don DeLillo and Paul Auster.

In *The Naked Lunch* (1959) and other novels William S. Burroughs, abandoning plot and coherent characterization, used a drug addict's consciousness to depict a hideous modern landscape.

William Seward Burroughs was an American writer of experimental novels that evoke, in deliberately erratic prose, a nightmarish, sometimes wildly humorous world. His sexual explicitness (he was an avowed and outspoken homosexual) and the frankness with which he dealt with his experiences as a drug addict won him a following among writers of the Beat movement.

Burroughs was born in 1914, the grandson of the inventor of the Burroughs adding machine. He grew up in St. Louis in comfortable circumstances, graduating from Harvard University in 1936 and continuing study there in archaeology and ethnology. Having tired of the academic world, he then held a variety of jobs. In 1943 Burroughs moved to New York City, where he became friends with Jack Kerouac and Allen Ginsberg, two writers who would become principal figures in the Beat movement. Burroughs first took morphine in about 1944, and he soon became addicted to heroin. That year Lucien Carr, a member of Burroughs's social circle, killed a man whom Carr claimed had made sexual advances toward him. Before turning himself in to the police, Carr confessed to Burroughs and Kerouac, who were both arrested as material witnesses. They were later released on bail, and neither man was charged with a crime. Carr was convicted of manslaughter but later pardoned. In 1945 Burroughs and Kerouac collaborated on a fictionalized retelling of those events entitled *And the Hippos Were Boiled in Their Tanks*. Rejected by publishers at the time, it was not published until 2008.

In 1949 he moved with his second wife to Mexico, where in 1951 he accidentally shot and killed her in a drunken prank. Fleeing Mexico, he wandered through the Amazon region of South America, continuing his experiments with drugs, a period of his life detailed in *The Yage Letters,* his correspondence with Ginsberg written in 1953 but not published until 1963. Between travels he lived in London, Paris, Tangier, and New York City but in 1981 settled in Lawrence, Kan., until his death in 1997.

He used the pen name William Lee in his first published book, *Junkie: Confessions of an Unredeemed Drug Addict* (1953; reissued as *Junky* in 1977), an account of the addict's life. *The Naked Lunch* (Paris, 1959; U.S. title, *Naked Lunch*, 1962; film 1991) was completed after his treatment for drug addiction. All forms of addiction, according to Burroughs, are counterproductive for writing, and the only gain to his own work from his 15 years as an addict came from the knowledge he acquired of the bizarre, carnival milieu in which the drug taker is preyed upon as victim. The grotesqueness of this world is vividly satirized in *The Naked Lunch*, which also is much preoccupied with homosexuality and police persecution. In the novels that followed—among them *The Soft Machine* (1961), *The Wild Boys* (1971), *Exterminator!* (1973), *Cities of the Red Night* (1981), *Place of Dead Roads* (1983), *Queer* (1985), *The Western Lands* (1987), and *My Education: A Book of Dreams* (1995)—Burroughs further experimented with the structure of the novel. *Burroughs* (1983), by filmmaker Howard Brookner, is a documentary on the artist's life.

In addition to Pynchon and Burroughs, Vonnegut, Terry Southern, and John Hawkes were also major practitioners of black humour and the absurdist fable. Other influential portraits of outsider figures included the Beat characters in Jack Kerouac's *On the Road* (1957), *The Dharma Bums* (1958), *Desolation Angels* (1965), and *Visions of Cody*

(1972); the young Rabbit Angstrom in John Updike's *Rabbit, Run* (1960) and *Rabbit Redux* (1971); Holden Caulfield in J.D. Salinger's *The Catcher in the Rye* (1951); and the troubling madman in Richard Yates's powerful novel of suburban life, *Revolutionary Road* (1961).

SOCIAL REALISM

Although writers such as Barth, Barthelme, and Pynchon rejected the novel's traditional function as a mirror reflecting society, a significant number of contemporary novelists were reluctant to abandon Social Realism, which they pursued in much more personal terms. In novels such as *The Victim* (1947), *The Adventures of Augie March* (1953), *Herzog* (1964), *Mr. Sammler's Planet* (1970), and *Humboldt's Gift* (1975), Saul Bellow tapped into the buoyant, manic energy and picaresque structure of black humour while proclaiming the necessity of "being human." Few contemporary writers saw the ugliness of urban life more clearly than Bellow, but his central characters rejected the "Wasteland outlook" that he associated with modernism.

Bellow's parents emigrated from Russia to Montreal in 1913, where he was born two years later. When he was nine years old, they moved to Chicago. He attended the University of Chicago and Northwestern University (B.S., 1937) and afterward combined writing with a teaching career at various universities, including the University of Minnesota, Princeton University, New York University, Bard College, the University of Chicago, and Boston University.

Bellow won a reputation among a small group of readers with his first two novels, *Dangling Man* (1944), a story in diary form of a man waiting to be inducted into the army, and *The Victim* (1947), a subtle study of the relationship between a Jew and a Gentile, each of whom becomes

Although he certainly had a knack for black humour, Saul Bellow also had a keen eye for the true face of urban life. Kevin Horan/Time & Life Pictures/ Getty Images

the other's victim. *The Adventures of Augie March* (1953) brought wider acclaim and won the National Book Award (1954). It is a picaresque story of a poor Jewish youth from Chicago, his progress—sometimes highly comic— through the world of the 20th century, and his attempts to make sense of it. In this novel Bellow employed for the first time a loose, breezy style in conscious revolt against the preoccupation of writers of that time with perfection of form.

Henderson the Rain King (1959) continued the picaresque approach in its tale of an eccentric American millionaire on a quest in Africa. The novella *Seize the Day* (1956) is a unique treatment of failure in a society where the only success is success. He also wrote a volume of short stories, *Mosby's Memoirs* (1968), and *To Jerusalem and Back* (1976) about a trip to Israel.

In his later novels and novellas—*Herzog* (1964; National Book Award, 1965), *Mr. Sammler's Planet* (1970;

National Book Award, 1971), *Humboldt's Gift* (1975; Pulitzer Prize, 1976), *The Dean's December* (1982), *More Die of Heartbreak* (1987), *A Theft* (1989), *The Bellarosa Connection* (1989), and *The Actual* (1997) — Bellow arrived at his most characteristic vein. The heroes of these works are often Jewish intellectuals whose interior monologues range from the sublime to the absurd. At the same time, their surrounding world, peopled by energetic and incorrigible realists, acts as a corrective to their intellectual specula-tions. It is this combination of cultural sophistication and the wisdom of the streets that constitutes Bellow's great-est originality. In *Ravelstein* (2000) he presented a fictional version of the life of teacher and philosopher Allan Bloom. Bellow died in 2005.

Four other major Jewish writers — Bernard Malamud, Grace Paley, Philip Roth, and Isaac Bashevis Singer — treated the human condition with humour and forgiveness. Malamud's gift for dark comedy and Hawthornean fable was especially evident in his short-story collections *The Magic Barrel* (1958) and *Idiots First* (1963). His first three novels, *The Natural* (1952), *The Assistant* (1957), and *A New Life* (1961), were also impressive works of fiction, but *The Assistant* had the bleak moral intensity of his best stories. Paley's stories combined an offbeat, whimsically poetic manner with a wry understanding of the ironies of family life and progressive politics. Although Roth was known best for the wild satire and sexual high jinks of *Portnoy's Complaint* (1969), a hilarious stand-up routine about eth-nic stereotypes, his most lasting achievement may be his later novels built around the misadventures of a contro-versial Jewish novelist named Zuckerman, especially *The Ghost Writer* (1979), *The Anatomy Lesson* (1983), and, above all, *The Counterlife* (1987).

Roth was born in Newark, N.J., in 1933. He received an M.A. from the University of Chicago and taught there and elsewhere. He first achieved fame with *Goodbye, Columbus* (1959; film 1969), whose title story candidly depicts the boorish materialism of a Jewish middle-class suburban family. Roth's first novel, *Letting Go* (1962), was followed in 1967 by *When She Was Good,* but he did not recapture the success of his first book until *Portnoy's Complaint* (1969; film 1972), an audacious satirical portrait of a contemporary Jewish male at odds with his domineering mother and obsessed with sexual experience. Several minor works, including *The Breast* (1972), *My Life As a Man* (1974), and *The Professor of Desire* (1977), were followed by one of Roth's most important novels, *The Ghost Writer* (1979), which introduced an aspiring young writer named Nathan Zuckerman. Roth's two subsequent novels, *Zuckerman Unbound* (1981) and *The Anatomy Lesson* (1983), trace his writer-protagonist's ensuing life and career and constitute Roth's first Zuckerman trilogy. These three novels were republished together with the novella *The Prague Orgy* under the title *Zuckerman Bound* (1985). A fourth Zuckerman novel, *The Counterlife,* appeared in 1993.

Roth was awarded a Pulitzer Prize for *American Pastoral* (1997), a novel about a middle-class couple whose daughter becomes a terrorist. It is the first novel of a second Zuckerman trilogy, completed by *I Married a Communist* (1998) and *The Human Stain* (2000; film 2003). In *The Dying Animal* (2001; filmed as *Elegy,* 2008), an aging literary professor reflects on a life of emotional isolation. *The Plot Against America* (2004) tells a counterhistorical story of fascism in the United States during World War II. With *Everyman* (2006), a novel that explores illness and death, Roth became the first three-time winner of the PEN/ Faulkner Award for Fiction, which he had won previously for *Operation Shylock* (1993) and *The Human Stain. Exit Ghost* (2007) revisits Zuckerman, who has been reawoken to life's possibilities after more than a decade of self-imposed exile in the Berkshire Mountains. *Indignation* (2008) is narrated from the afterlife by a man who died at age 19. The novella *The Humbling* (2009) revisits *Everyman*'s mortality-obsessed terrain, this time through the lens of an aging actor who, realizing that he has lost his talent, finds himself unable to work.

The Polish-born Isaac Bashevis Singer won the Nobel Prize for Literature in 1978 for his stories, written originally in Yiddish. They evolved from fantastic tales of demons and angels to realistic fictions set in New York City's Upper West Side, often dealing with the haunted lives of Holocaust survivors. These works showed him to be one of the great storytellers of modern times.

Singer was born in 1904. His birth date is uncertain and has been variously reported as July 14, November 21, and October 26. He came from a family of Hasidic rabbis on his father's side and a long line of Mitnagdic rabbis on his mother's side. He received a traditional Jewish education at the Warsaw Rabbinical Seminary. His older brother was the novelist I.J. Singer and his sister the writer Esther Kreytman (Kreitman). Like his brother, Singer preferred being a writer to being a rabbi. In 1925 he made his debut with the story "Af der elter" ("In Old Age"), which he published in the Warsaw *Literarishe bleter* under a pseudonym. His first novel, *Der Sotn in Goray* (*Satan in Goray*), was published in installments in Poland shortly before he immigrated to the United States in 1935.

Settling in New York City, as his brother had done a year earlier, Singer worked for the Yiddish newspaper *Forverts* (*Jewish Daily Forward*), and as a journalist he signed his articles with the pseudonym Varshavski or D. Segal. He also translated many books into Yiddish from

Isaac Bashevis Singer's works ranged from wild tales of the fantastic to realistic stories of Holocaust survivors set in New York City. Nancy Rica Schiff/ Time & Life Pictures/Getty Images

Hebrew, Polish, and, particularly, German, among them works by Thomas Mann and Erich Maria Remarque. In 1943 he became a U.S. citizen.

Although Singer's works became most widely known in their English versions, he continued to write almost exclusively in Yiddish, personally supervising the translations. The relationship between his works in these two languages is complex: Some novels and short stories were published in Yiddish in the *Forverts*, for which he wrote until his death, and then appeared in book form only in English translation. However, some later also appeared in book form in the original Yiddish after the success of the English translation. Among his most important novels are *The Family Moskat* (1950; *Di familye Mushkat*, 1950), *The Magician of Lublin* (1960; *Der kuntsnmakher fun Lublin*, 1971), and *The Slave* (1962; *Der knekht*, 1967). *The Manor* (1967) and *The Estate* (1969) are based on *Der hoyf*, serialized in the *Forverts* in 1953–55. *Enemies: A Love Story* (1972; film 1989) was translated from *Sonim: di geshikhte fun a libe*, serialized in the *Forverts* in 1966. *Shosha*, derived from autobiographical material Singer published in the *Forverts* in the mid-1970s, appeared in English in 1978. *Der bal-tshuve* (1974) was published first in book form in Yiddish and later translated into English as *The Penitent* (1983). *Shadows on the Hudson*, translated into English and published posthumously in 1998, is a novel on a grand scale about Jewish refugees in New York in the late 1940s. The book had been serialized in the *Forverts* in the 1950s.

Singer's popular collections of short stories in English translation include *Gimpel the Fool, and Other Stories* (1957; *Gimpl tam, un andere dertseylungen*, 1963), *The Spinoza of Market Street* (1961), *Short Friday* (1964), *The Seance* (1968), *A Crown of Feathers* (1973; National Book Award), *Old Love* (1979), and *The Image, and Other Stories* (1985).

Singer evokes in his writings the vanished world of Polish Jewry as it existed before the Holocaust. His most ambitious novels—*The Family Moskat* and the continuous narrative spun out in *The Manor* and *The Estate*—have large casts of characters and extend over several generations. These books chronicle the changes in, and eventual breakup of, large Jewish families during the late 19th and early 20th centuries as their members are differently affected by the secularism and assimilationist opportunities of the modern era. Singer's shorter novels examine characters variously tempted by evil, such as the brilliant circus magician of *The Magician of Lublin*, the 17th-century Jewish villagers crazed by messianism in *Satan in Goray*, and the enslaved Jewish scholar in *The Slave*. His short stories are saturated with Jewish folklore, legends, and mysticism and display his incisive understanding of the weaknesses inherent in human nature.

Schlemiel Went to Warsaw, and Other Stories (1968) is one of his best-known books for children. In 1966 he published *In My Father's Court*, based on the Yiddish *Mayn tatns besdn shtub* (1956), an autobiographical account of his childhood in Warsaw. This work received special praise from the Swedish Academy when Singer was awarded the Nobel Prize. *More Stories from My Father's Court*, posthumously published in 2000 (Singer died in 1991), includes childhood stories Singer had first published in the *Forverts* in the 1950s. His memoir *Love and Exile* appeared in 1984.

Several films have been adapted from Singer's works, including *The Magician of Lublin* (1979), based on his novel of the same name, and *Yentl* (1983), based on his story "Yentl" in *Mayses fun hintern oyvn* (1971; "Stories from Behind the Stove").

Another great storyteller of the post-World War II era, John Cheever, long associated with the *New Yorker* magazine, created in his short stories and novels a gallery of

The New Yorker

The *New Yorker* is an American weekly magazine, famous for its varied literary fare and humour. The founder, Harold W. Ross, published the first issue on Feb. 21, 1925, and was the magazine's editor until his death in December 1951. The *New Yorker*'s initial focus was on New York City's amusements and social and cultural life, but the magazine gradually acquired a broader scope that encompassed literature, current affairs, and other topics. The *New Yorker* became renowned for its short fiction, essays, foreign reportage, and probing biographical studies, as well as its comic drawings and its detailed reviews of cinema, books, theatre, and other arts. The magazine offered a blend of reportage and commentary, short stories and poetry, reviews, and humour to a sophisticated, well-educated, liberal audience.

The *New Yorker*'s contributors have included such well-known literary figures as S.J. Perelman, Robert Benchley, Ogden Nash, E.B. White, John O'Hara, Edmund Wilson, J.D. Salinger, John Cheever, John Updike, Rebecca West, Dorothy Parker, Alice Munro, Jane Kramer, Woody Allen, John McPhee, and Milan Kundera. Among its great cartoonists have been Charles Addams, Helen Hokinson, George Price, James Thurber (a writer as well), Roz Chast, Saul Steinberg, Gahan Wilson, William Steig, Edward Koren, and Rea Irvin, who was the magazine's first art director and the creator of Eustace Tilley, the early American dandy (inspired by an illustration in the 11th edition of *Encyclopædia Britannica*) who appeared on the cover of the first issue and on annual covers thereafter.

In 1985 the *New Yorker* was sold to the publisher Samuel I. Newhouse, Jr., this being the first time in its history that the magazine's ownership had changed hands. William Shawn was the magazine's editor in chief from 1952 to 1987, when he was succeeded by Robert Gottlieb, formerly a book editor and executive at Alfred A. Knopf publishers. In 1992 a Briton, Tina Brown, formerly editor of *Vanity Fair*, replaced Gottlieb. Under Brown's editorship, cosmetic changes to the magazine's traditionally conservative layout were introduced, coverage of popular culture was enhanced, and more photographs were published. In 1998 Brown left the magazine and was replaced by staff writer David Remnick. The *New Yorker* continued to attract leading writers and remained among the most influential and widely read American magazines.

memorable eccentrics. He has been called "the Chekhov of the suburbs" for his ability to capture the drama and sadness of the lives of his characters by revealing the undercurrents of apparently insignificant events.

Cheever was born in 1912 into a middle-class family in New England, where his father was employed in the then-booming shoe business. With the eventual failure of the shoe industry and the difficulties of his parents' marriage, he had an unhappy adolescence. His expulsion at age 17 from the Thayer Academy in Massachusetts provided the theme for his first published story, which appeared in the *New Republic* in 1930. During the Great Depression he lived in New York City's Greenwich Village. Cheever married in 1941 and had three children. In 1942 he enlisted in the army to train as an infantryman, but the army soon reassigned him to the Signal Corps as a scriptwriter for training films. After the war Cheever and his wife moved from New York City to the suburbs, whose culture and mores are often examined in his subsequent fiction.

Cheever's name was closely associated with the *New Yorker*, but his works also appeared in the *New Republic*, *Collier's*, *Story*, and the *Atlantic Monthly*. A master of the short story, Cheever worked from "the interrupted event," which he considered the prime source of short stories. He was famous for his clear and elegant prose and his careful fashioning of incidents and anecdotes. He is perhaps best known for the two stories "The Enormous Radio" (1947) and "The Swimmer" (1964; film 1968). In the former story, a young couple discovers that their new radio receives the conversations of other people in their apartment building, but this fascinating look into other people's problems does not solve their own. In "The Swimmer" a suburban man decides to swim his way home in the backyard pools of his neighbours, and along the way he realizes he is a lost soul in several senses. Cheever's first collection of short stories, *The Way Some People Live* (1943), was followed by many others, including *The Enormous Radio and Other Stories* (1953) and *The Brigadier and the Golf Widow* (1964). *The Stories of John Cheever* (1978) won the Pulitzer Prize for fiction.

Cheever's ability in his short stories to focus on the episodic caused him difficulty in constructing extended narratives in his novels. Nonetheless, his first novel, *The Wapshot Chronicle* (1957)—a satire on, among other subjects, the misuses of wealth and psychology—earned him the National Book Award. Its sequel, *The Wapshot Scandal* (1964), was less successful. *Falconer* (1977) is the dark tale of a drug-addicted college professor who is imprisoned for murdering his brother. The elegiac *Oh What a Paradise It Seems* (1982) is a novel about a New Englander's efforts to preserve the quality of his life and that of a mill town's pond. Cheever died in 1982, and *The Letters of John Cheever* (1988; edited by his son Benjamin Cheever) and *The Journals of John Cheever* (1991) were published posthumously. The latter is deeply revealing of both the man and the writer, wherein Cheever was shown to have struggled greatly with his alcoholism and secret bisexuality.

The sexual and moral confusion of the American middle class was the focus of the work of J.D. Salinger and Richard Yates, as well as of John Updike's Rabbit series (four novels from *Rabbit, Run* [1960] to *Rabbit at Rest*

John Updike

(b. March 18, 1932, Reading, Penn.—d. Jan. 27, 2009, Danvers, Mass.)

John Updike wrote novels, short stories, and poetry and was known for his careful craftsmanship and realistic but subtle depiction of "American, Protestant, small-town, middle-class" life.

Updike grew up in Shillington, Penn., and many of his early stories draw on his youthful experiences there. He graduated from Harvard University in 1954. In 1955 he began an association with the *New Yorker* magazine, to which he contributed editorials, poetry, stories, and criticism throughout his prolific career. His poetry—intellectual, witty pieces on the absurdities of modern life—was gathered in his first book, *The Carpentered Hen and Other Tame Creatures* (1958), which was followed by his first novel, *The Poorhouse Fair* (1958). About this time, Updike devoted himself to writing fiction full time, and several works followed. *Rabbit, Run* (1960), which is considered to be one of his best novels, concerns a former star athlete who is unable to recapture success when bound by marriage and small-town life and flees responsibility. Three subsequent novels, *Rabbit Redux* (1971), *Rabbit Is Rich* (1981), and *Rabbit at Rest* (1990)—the latter two winning Pulitzer Prizes—follow the same character during later periods of his life. *Rabbit Remembered* (2001) returns to characters from those books in the wake of Rabbit's death. *The Centaur* (1963) and *Of the Farm* (1965) are notable among Updike's novels set in Pennsylvania.

Much of Updike's later fiction is set in New England (in Ipswich, Mass.), where he lived from the 1960s. Updike continued to explore the issues that confront middle-class America, such as fidelity, religion, and responsibility. The novels *Couples* (1968) and *Marry Me* (1976) expose the evolving sexual politics of the time in East Coast suburbia. Updike set *Memories of the Ford Administration: A Novel* (1992) in the 1970s, infusing the tale of a professor's research on Pres. James Buchanan with observations on sexuality. *In the Beauty of the Lilies* (1996) draws parallels between religion and popular obsession with cinema, whereas

Gertrude and Claudius (2000) offers conjectures on the early relationship between Hamlet's mother and her brother-in-law. In response to the cultural shifts that occurred in the United States after the September 11 attacks, Updike released *Terrorist* in 2006.

Updike often expounded upon characters from earlier novels, eliding decades of their lives only to place them in the middle of new adventures. *The Witches of Eastwick* (1984; film 1987), about a coven of witches, was followed by *The Widows of Eastwick* (2008), which trails the women into old age. *Bech: A Book* (1970), *Bech Is Back* (1982), and *Bech at Bay* (1998) humorously trace the tribulations of a Jewish writer.

Updike's several collections of short stories include *The Same Door* (1959), *Pigeon Feathers* (1962), *Museums and Women* (1972), *Problems* (1979), *Trust Me* (1987), and *My Father's Tears, and Other Stories* (2009), which was published posthumously. He also wrote nonfiction and criticism, much of it appearing in the *New Yorker,* which has been collected in *Assorted Prose* (1965), *Picked-Up Pieces* (1975), *Hugging the Shore* (1983), and *Odd Jobs* (1991). *Still Looking: Essays on American Art* (2005) examines both art and its cultural presentation, and *Due Considerations* (2007) collects later commentary spanning art, sexuality, and literature. Updike also continued to write poetry, usually light verse. His own death was a primary subject in the posthumously published *Endpoint, and Other Poems* (2009), which collects poetry Updike wrote between 2002 and a few weeks before he died.

[1990]), *Couples* (1968), and *Too Far to Go* (1979), a sequence of tales about the quiet disintegration of a civilized marriage, a subject Updike revisited in a retrospective work, *Villages* (2004). In sharp contrast, Nelson Algren (*The Man with the Golden Arm* [1949]) and Hubert Selby, Jr. (*Last Exit to Brooklyn* [1964]), documented lower-class urban life with brutal frankness. Similarly, John Rechy portrayed America's urban homosexual subculture in *City of Night* (1963).

SOUTHERN FICTION

Post–World War II Southern writers inherited William Faulkner's rich legacy. Three women—Eudora Welty, Flannery O'Connor, and Carson McCullers—specialists in the grotesque, contributed greatly to Southern fiction.

Eudora Welty was born in 1909 in Jackson, Miss. She attended Mississippi State College for Women before transferring to the University of Wisconsin, from which she graduated in 1929. During the Great Depression she was a photographer on the Works Progress Administration's guide to Mississippi, and photography remained a lifelong interest. *Photographs* (1989) is a collection of many of the photographs she took for the WPA. She also worked as a writer for a radio station and newspaper in her native Jackson, Miss., before her fiction won popular and critical acclaim.

Welty's first short story was published in 1936, and thereafter her work began to appear regularly, first in little magazines such as the *Southern Review* and later in major periodicals such as the *Atlantic Monthly* and *The New Yorker*. Her readership grew steadily after the publication of *A Curtain of Green* (1941; enlarged 1979), a volume of short stories that contains two of her most anthologized stories—"The Petrified Man" and "Why I Live at the P.O." In 1942 her short novel *The Robber Bridegroom* was issued, and in 1946 her first full-length novel, *Delta Wedding,*was published. Her later novels include *The Ponder Heart* (1954), *Losing Battles* (1970), and *The Optimist's Daughter* (1972), which won a Pulitzer Prize. *The Wide Net and Other Stories* (1943), *The Golden Apples* (1949), and *The Bride of Innisfallen and Other Stories* (1955) are collections of short stories, and *The Eye of the Story* (1978) is a volume of essays. *The Collected Stories of Eudora Welty* was published in 1980.

Welty's main subject is the intricacies of human relationships, particularly as revealed through her characters' interactions in intimate social encounters. Among her themes are the subjectivity and ambiguity of people's perception of character and the presence of virtue hidden beneath an obscuring surface of convention, insensitivity, and social prejudice. Welty's outlook is hopeful, and love is viewed as a redeeming presence in the midst of isolation and indifference. Her works combine humour and psychological acuity with a sharp ear for regional speech patterns.

One Writer's Beginnings, an autobiographical work, was published in 1984. Originating in a series of three lectures given at Harvard, it beautifully evoked what Welty styled her "sheltered life" in Jackson and how her early fiction grew out of it. Welty died in 2001.

Flannery O'Connor was born in 1925, and she grew up in a prominent Roman Catholic family in her native Georgia. She lived in Savannah until her adolescence, when the worsening of her father's lupus erythematosus forced the family to relocate in 1938 to her mother's childhood home in rural Milledgeville. After graduating from Georgia State College for Women (now Georgia College & State University) in 1945, she studied creative writing at the University of Iowa Writers' Workshop.

Her first published work, a short story, appeared in the magazine *Accent* in 1946. Her first novel, *Wise Blood* (1952; film 1979), explored, in O'Connor's own words, the "religious consciousness without a religion." *Wise Blood* consists of a series of near-independent chapters—many of which originated in previously published short stories—that tell the tale of Hazel Motes, a man who returns home from military service and founds the Church Without Christ, which leads to a series of interactions with

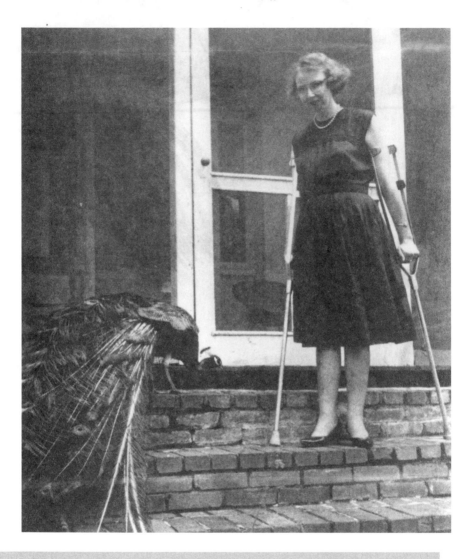

Flannery O'Connor. Library of Congress, Washington, D.C.; neg. no.
LC USZ 62 108013

the grotesque inhabitants of his hometown. The work
combines the keen ear for common speech, caustic religious imagination, and flair for the absurd that were to
characterize her subsequent work. With the publication
of further short stories, first collected in *A Good Man Is*

Hard to Find, and Other Stories (1955), she came to be regarded as a master of the form. The collection's eponymous story has become possibly her best-known work. In it O'Connor creates an unexpected agent of salvation in the character of an escaped convict called The Misfit, who kills a quarreling family on vacation in the Deep South.

Her other works of fiction are a novel, *The Violent Bear It Away* (1960), and the short-story collection *Everything That Rises Must Converge* (1965). A collection of occasional prose pieces, *Mystery and Manners*, appeared in 1969. Published posthumously in 1971, *The Complete Stories* contained several stories that had not previously appeared in book form, and it won a National Book Award in 1972.

Disabled for more than a decade by the lupus erythematosus she inherited from her father, which eventually proved fatal, O'Connor lived modestly, writing and raising peafowl on her mother's farm at Milledgeville. After her death in 1964, the posthumous publication of her letters, under the title *The Habit of Being* (1979), and her book reviews and correspondence with local diocesan newspapers, published as *The Presence of Grace, and Other Book Reviews* (1983), provided valuable insight into the life and mind of a writer whose works defy conventional categorization. O'Connor's corpus is notable for the seeming incongruity of a devout Catholic whose darkly comic works commonly feature startling acts of violence and unsympathetic, often depraved, characters. She explained the prevalence of brutality in her stories by noting that violence "is strangely capable of returning my characters to reality and preparing them to accept their moment of grace." It is this divine stripping of man's comforts and hubris, along with the attendant degradation of the corporeal, that stands as the most salient feature of O'Connor's work.

Carson McCullers was born Lula Carson Smith in Columbus, Ga., in 1917. At age 17 she went to New York

City to study at Columbia and New York universities, and in 1937 she married Reeves McCullers, a writer whom she had met in Georgia and with whom she was to have a long and complicated relationship. They divorced in 1940 after he was found to have forged some of her royalty checks but remarried in 1945. Her life after that was clouded by pain, illness, and tragedy. She fell in love at least twice with women who did not reciprocate her feelings and once with a man who also interested her husband. Repeated strokes incapacitated her for long periods, and partial paralysis confined McCullers to a wheelchair in her later years.

Her achievement as a writer—a career that was successfully launched by her first novel, *The Heart Is a Lonely Hunter* (1940; film 1968)—was the outgrowth of her own character and lonely suffering. The novel concerns four inhabitants of a small town in Georgia—an adolescent girl with a passion to study music, an unsuccessful socialist agitator, a black physician struggling to maintain his personal dignity, and a widower who owns a café. *Reflections in a Golden Eye* (1941; film 1967), a shorter work set in a Southern army post that chronicles the unhappy life of a captain (a latent homosexual) and his wife (a nymphomaniac), confirmed McCullers's earlier success.

During the 1940s McCullers met American playwright Tennessee Williams, and they became friends. Williams encouraged her to make a play of her novel *The Member of the Wedding* (1946), a sensitive portrayal of a lonely adolescent whose attachment to her brother precipitates a crisis at his wedding. The novel proved to be her most popular work, and it was equally successful as a play, heralded by some as a new form of American theatre because of its emphasis on character interaction and psychology. The Broadway version ran for more than a year and was made into a movie in 1952.

The fictional characters McCullers creates endure various physical and psychological handicaps that complicate their natural but often bizarre searches for compassion. Her novels and stories demonstrate a Southern gothic embrace of the eccentric and combine examinations of relationships between people, reflections on such subjects as the inherent incompatibility of the lover and the beloved, and a profound sense of the human longing to connect with others. She felt her characters powerfully, once stating that "I live with the people I create and it has always made my essential loneliness less keen." Her other works include *The Ballad of the Sad Café* (1951), the drama *The Square Root of Wonderful* (1958), and the novel *Clock Without Hands* (1961). McCullers died in 1967. Her *Collected Stories* appeared posthumously in 1987, and *Illumination and Night Glare: The Unfinished Autobiography of Carson McCullers*, segmented and with large lacunae, was published in 1999.

Other fine storytellers in the Southern tradition include Elizabeth Spencer, whose short fiction was collected in *The Southern Woman* (2001), and Reynolds Price, whose best novels were *A Long and Happy Life* (1961) and *Kate Vaiden* (1986). Initially known for his lyrical portraits of Southern eccentrics (*Other Voices, Other Rooms* [1948]), Truman Capote later published *In Cold Blood* (1966), a cold but impressive piece of documentary realism that contributed, along with the work of Tom Wolfe and Norman Mailer, to the emergence of a "new journalism" that used many of the techniques of fiction.

William Styron's overripe first novel, *Lie Down in Darkness* (1951), clearly revealed the influence of Faulkner. In two controversial later works, Styron fictionalized the dark side of modern history: *The Confessions of Nat Turner* (1967) depicted an antebellum slave revolt, and *Sophie's Choice* (1979) unsuccessfully sought to capture the full

Truman Capote

(b. Sept. 30, 1924, New Orleans, La., — d. Aug. 25, 1984, Los Angeles, Calif.)

Truman Capote was a novelist, short-story writer, and playwright. His early writing extended the Southern Gothic tradition, but he later developed a more journalistic approach in the novel *In Cold Blood* (1965), which remains his best-known work.

Born Truman Persons, his parents divorced when he was young, and he spent his childhood with various elderly relatives in small towns in Louisiana and Alabama. (He owed his surname to his mother's remarriage, to Joseph Garcia Capote.) He attended private schools and eventually joined his mother and stepfather in Millbrook, Conn., where he completed his secondary education at Greenwich High School.

Capote drew on his childhood experiences for much of his early fiction. Having abandoned further schooling, he achieved early literary recognition in 1945 when his haunting short story "Miriam" was published in *Mademoiselle* magazine. It won the O. Henry Memorial Award the following year, the first of four such awards Capote was to receive. His first novel, *Other Voices, Other Rooms* (1948), was acclaimed as the work of a young writer of great promise. The book is a sensitive portrayal of a homosexually inclined boy's search for his father and his own identity through a nightmarishly decadent Southern world. The short story "Shut a Final Door" (O. Henry Award, 1946) and other tales of loveless and isolated persons were collected in *A Tree of Night* (1949). The quasi-autobiographical novel *The Grass Harp* (1951) is a story of nonconforming innocents who retire temporarily from life to a tree house, returning renewed to the real world. One of Capote's most popular works, *Breakfast at Tiffany's* (1958; film 1961), is a novella about a young, fey Manhattan playgirl.

Capote's increasing preoccupation with journalism was reflected in the "nonfiction novel" *In Cold Blood,* a chilling account of a multiple murder committed by two young psychopaths in Kansas. Capote spent six years interviewing the principals in the case, and the critical and popular success of his novel about them was the high point of his dual careers as a writer and a celebrity socialite. Although a serious writer, Capote was also a party-loving sybarite who became a darling of the rich and famous of high society. Endowed with a quirky but attractive character, he entertained television audiences with outrageous tales recounted in his distinctively high-pitched Southern drawl.

Capote's later writings never approached the success of his earlier ones. In the late 1960s he adapted two short stories about his childhood, "A Christmas Memory" and "The Thanksgiving Visitor," for television. *The Dogs Bark* (1973) consists of collected essays and profiles over a 30-year span, while the collection *Music for Chameleons* (1980) includes both fiction and nonfiction. In later years Capote's growing dependence on drugs and alcohol stifled his productivity. Moreover, selections from a projected work that he considered to be his masterpiece, a social satire entitled *Answered Prayers,* appeared in *Esquire* magazine in 1975 and raised a storm among friends and foes who were harshly depicted in the work (under the thinnest of disguises). He was thereafter ostracized by his former celebrity friends, and *Answered Prayers* remained unfinished at his death.

horror of the Holocaust. Inspired by Faulkner and Mark Twain, William Humphrey wrote two powerful novels set in Texas, *Home from the Hill* (1958) and *The Ordways* (1965). *The Moviegoer* (1961) and *The Last Gentleman* (1966) established Walker Percy as an important voice in Southern fiction. The musing philosophical style of Percy's novels broke sharply with the Southern gothic tradition and influenced later writers such as Richard Ford in *The Sportswriter* (1986) and its moving sequel, *Independence Day* (1995). Equally impressive were the novels and stories of Peter Taylor, an impeccable Social Realist, raconteur, and genial novelist of manners who recalled a bygone world in works such as *The Old Forest* (1985) and *A Summons to Memphis* (1986).

Walker Percy

(b. May 28, 1916, Birmingham, Ala. —d. May 10, 1990, Covington, La.)

The novelist Walker Percy wrote of the New South transformed by industry and technology.

Orphaned in late childhood after his father, a lawyer, committed suicide and his mother died in an automobile accident, Percy went with his brothers to live with their father's cousin, a bachelor and lawyer, in Greenville, Miss. Percy studied at the University of North Carolina (B.A., 1937) and Columbia University (M.D., 1941) and, while working as a pathologist at Bellevue Hospital, New York City, contracted tuberculosis, compelling him to rest at an upstate New York sanatorium. While recovering, he read widely, was attracted to the works of European existentialists, and decided on a career in writing. He also converted to Roman Catholicism.

During the 1950s Percy wrote articles for philosophical, literary, and psychiatric journals. Finally, in 1961 his first novel was published, *The Moviegoer*, which won a National Book Award and introduced Percy's concept of "malaise," a disease of despair born of the rootless modern world. Other fiction included *The Last Gentleman* (1966), *Love in the Ruins: The Adventures of a Bad Catholic at a Time Near the End of the World* (1971), *Lancelot* (1977), *The Second Coming* (1980), and *The Thanatos Syndrome* (1987). He also wrote such nonfiction as *The Message in the Bottle* (1975), a sophisticated philosophical treatment of semantics.

AFRICAN AMERICAN LITERATURE

Black writers of this period found alternatives to the Richard Wright tradition of angry social protest. James Baldwin and Ralph Ellison, both protégés of Wright, wrote polemical essays calling for a literature that reflected the full complexity of black life in the United States.

James Baldwin was born in 1924. The eldest of nine children, he grew up in poverty in the black ghetto of Harlem in New York City. From 14 to 16 years of age he was active during out-of-school hours as a preacher in a small revivalist church, a period he wrote about in his semiautobiographical first and finest novel, *Go Tell It on the Mountain* (1953), and in his play about a woman evangelist, *The Amen Corner* (performed in New York City, 1965).

After graduation from high school, he began a restless period of ill-paid jobs, self-study, and literary apprenticeship in Greenwich Village, the bohemian quarter of New York City. He left for Paris in 1948, where he lived for the next eight years. (In later years, from 1969, he became a self-styled "transatlantic commuter," living alternatively in the south of France and in New York and New England.) His second novel, *Giovanni's Room* (1956), deals with the white world and concerns an American in Paris torn between his love for a man and his love for a woman. Between the two novels came a collection of essays, *Notes of a Native Son* (1955).

In 1957 he returned to the United States and became an active participant in the civil rights struggle that swept the nation. His book of essays, *Nobody Knows My Name* (1961), explores black–white relations in the United States. This theme also was central to his novel *Another Country* (1962), which examines sexual as well as racial issues.

The *New Yorker* magazine gave over almost all of its Nov. 17, 1962, issue to a long article by Baldwin on the Black Muslim separatist movement and other aspects of the civil rights struggle. The article became a best seller in book form as *The Fire Next Time* (1963). His bitter play about racist oppression, *Blues for Mister Charlie* ("Mister Charlie" being a black term for a white man), played on Broadway to mixed reviews in 1964.

Baldwin continued to write until his death in 1987. He published works including *Going to Meet the Man* (1965), a collection of short stories; and the novels *Tell Me How Long the Train's Been Gone* (1968), *If Beale Street Could Talk* (1974), and *Just Above My Head* (1979); and *The Price of the Ticket* (1985), a collection of autobiographical writings. However, none of his later works achieved the popular and critical success of his early work.

Drawing on rural folktale, absurdist humour, and a picaresque realism, Ralph Ellison wrote a deeply resonant comic novel that dealt with the full range of black experience—rural sharecropping, segregated education, northward migration, ghetto hustling, and the lure of such competing ideologies as nationalism and communism. Many considered his novel *Invisible Man* (1952) the best novel of the postwar years.

Ellison was born in 1914 in Oklahoma City, Okla. He left Tuskegee Normal and Industrial Institute (now Tuskegee University) in 1936 after three years' study of music and moved to New York City. There he befriended Richard Wright, who encouraged him to try his hand at writing. In 1937 Ellison began contributing short stories, reviews, and essays to various periodicals. He worked on the Federal Writers' Project from 1938 to 1942, which he followed with a stint as the managing editor of the *Negro Quarterly* for just less than a year.

Following service in World War II, he produced *Invisible Man*, which won the 1953 National Book Award for fiction. The story is a bildungsroman that tells of a naive and idealistic (and, significantly, nameless) Southern black youth who goes to Harlem, joins the fight against white oppression, and ends up ignored by his fellow blacks as well as by whites. The novel won praise for its stylistic innovations in infusing classic literary motifs with modern black speech and culture, while providing a thoroughly unique take on the construction of contemporary African American identity. However, Ellison's treatment of his novel as first and foremost a work of art—as opposed to a primarily polemical work—led to some complaints from his fellow black novelists at the time that he was not sufficiently devoted to social change.

After *Invisible Man* appeared, Ellison published only two collections of essays: *Shadow and Act* (1964) and *Going to the Territory* (1986). He lectured widely on black culture, folklore, and creative writing and taught at various American colleges and universities until his death in 1994. *Flying Home and Other Stories* was published posthumously in 1996. He left a second novel unfinished at his death, which was published, in a much-shortened form, as *Juneteenth* in 1999.

Later two African American women—Toni Morrison and Alice Walker—published some of the most important post–World War II American fiction. In *The Bluest Eye* (1970), *Sula* (1973), *Song of Solomon* (1977), *Beloved* (1987), *Jazz* (1992), and *Paradise* (1998), Morrison created a strikingly original fiction that sounded different notes from lyrical recollection to magic realism. Like Ellison, Morrison drew on diverse literary and folk influences and dealt with important phases of black history—i.e., slavery in *Beloved* and the Harlem Renaissance in *Jazz*. She was awarded the Nobel Prize for Literature in 1993.

Born Chloe Anthony Wofford in 1931, Morrison grew up in the American Midwest in a family that possessed an intense love of and appreciation for black culture. Storytelling, songs, and folktales were a deeply formative part of her childhood. She attended Howard University (B.A., 1953) and Cornell University (M.A., 1955). After teaching at Texas Southern University for two years, she taught at Howard from 1957 to 1964, where she married and began to be known as Toni Morrison. In 1965 she became a fiction editor. From 1984 she taught writing at the State University of New York at Albany, leaving in 1989 to join the faculty of Princeton University.

Morrison's first book, *The Bluest Eye* (1970), is a novel of initiation concerning a victimized adolescent black girl who is obsessed by white standards of beauty and longs to have blue eyes. In 1973 *Sula* was published. Morrison's second work, it examines (among other issues) the dynamics of friendship and the expectations for conformity within the community. *Song of Solomon* (1977) is told by a male narrator in search of his identity, and its publication brought Morrison to national attention. *Tar Baby* (1981), set on a Caribbean island, explores conflicts of race, class, and sex. The critically acclaimed *Beloved* (1987), which won a Pulitzer Prize for fiction, is based on the true story of a runaway slave who, at the point of recapture, kills her infant daughter to spare her a life of slavery. *Jazz* (1992) is a story of violence and passion set in New York City's Harlem during the 1920s. Subsequent novels are *Paradise* (1998), a richly detailed portrait of a black utopian community in Oklahoma, *Love* (2003), an intricate family story that reveals the myriad facets of love and its ostensible opposite, and *A Mercy* (2008), which deals with slavery in 17th-century America.

A work of criticism, *Playing in the Dark: Whiteness and the Literary Imagination*, was published in 1992. Many of her essays and speeches were collected in *What Moves at the Margin: Selected Nonfiction* (edited by Carolyn C. Denard), published in 2008. Additionally, Morrison released several children's books, including *Who's Got Game?: The Ant or the Grasshopper?* and *Who's Got Game?: The Lion or the Mouse?*, both written with her son and published in 2003. *Remember* (2004) chronicles the hardships of black students during the integration of the American public school system. Aimed at children, it uses archival photographs juxtaposed with captions speculating on the thoughts of their subjects. She also wrote the libretto for

Margaret Garner (2005), an opera about the same story that inspired *Beloved*.

The central theme of Morrison's novels is the black American experience. In an unjust society, her characters struggle to find themselves and their cultural identity. Her use of fantasy, her sinuous poetic style, and her rich interweaving of the mythic gave her stories great strength and texture.

Magic Realism

Magic realism is a chiefly Latin American narrative strategy that is characterized by the matter-of-fact inclusion of fantastic or mythical elements into seemingly realistic fiction. Although this strategy is known in the literature of many cultures in many ages, the term "magic realism" is a relatively recent designation, first applied in the 1940s by Cuban novelist Alejo Carpentier, who recognized this characteristic in much Latin American literature. Some scholars have posited that magic realism is a natural outcome of postcolonial writing, which must make sense of at least two separate realities—the reality of the conquerors as well as that of the conquered. Prominent among the Latin American magic realists are the Colombian Gabriel García Márquez, the Brazilian Jorge Amado, the Argentines Jorge Luis Borges and Julio Cortazar, and the Chilean Isabel Allende. The influence of magic realism as practiced by these writers was international in scope and can be seen in works by Toni Morrison, Maxine Hong Kingston, and many other American writers working during the second half of the 20th century.

Another important African American writer of the post–World War II era is Alice Walker, whose novels, short stories, and poems are noted for their insightful treatment of African American culture. Her novels, most notably *The Color Purple* (1982), particularly focus on women.

Alice Walker's thoughtful novels, short stories, and poems resonate with folklore, offering particular insight into the lives of African American women.
Justin Sullivan/Getty Images

Born in 1944, Walker was the eighth child of African American sharecroppers in rural Georgia. While growing up she was accidentally blinded in one eye, and her mother gave her a typewriter, allowing her to write instead of doing chores. She received a scholarship to attend Spelman College, where she studied for two years before transferring to Sarah Lawrence College. After graduating in 1965, Walker moved to Mississippi and became involved in the civil rights movement. She also began teaching and publishing short stories and essays. She married in 1967, but the couple divorced in 1976.

Walker's first book of poetry, *Once*, appeared in 1968, and her first novel, *The Third Life of Grange Copeland* (1970), a narrative that spans 60 years and three generations, followed two years later. A second volume of poetry, *Revolutionary Petunias and Other Poems*, and her first collection of short stories, *In Love and Trouble: Stories of Black Women*, both appeared in 1973. The latter bears witness to sexist violence and abuse in the African American community. After moving to New York, Walker completed *Meridian* (1976), a novel describing the coming of age of several civil rights workers in the 1960s.

Walker later moved to California, where she wrote her most popular novel, *The Color Purple* (1982). An epistolary novel, it depicts the growing up and self-realization of an African American woman between 1909 and 1947 in a town in Georgia. The book won a Pulitzer Prize and was adapted into a film by Steven Spielberg in 1985. A musical version produced by Oprah Winfrey and Quincy Jones premiered in 2004.

Walker's later fiction includes *The Temple of My Familiar*, an ambitious examination of racial and sexual tensions (1989); *Possessing the Secret of Joy* (1992), a narrative centred on female genital mutilation; *By the Light of My Father's Smile* (1998), the story of a family of anthropologists posing as missionaries to gain access to a Mexican tribe; and *Now Is the Time to Open Your Heart* (2005), about an older woman's quest for identity. Reviewers complained that these novels employed New Age abstractions and poorly conceived characters, but Walker continued to draw praise for championing racial and gender equality in her work. She also released the volume of short stories *The Way Forward Is with a Broken Heart* (2000) and several other volumes of poetry, including *Absolute Trust in the Goodness of the Earth* (2003) and *A Poem Traveled Down My Arm* (2003). *Her Blue Body Everything We Know: Earthling Poems* (1991) collects poetry from 1965 to 1990.

Her essays were compiled in *In Search of Our Mother's Gardens: Womanist Prose* (1983), *Sent by Earth: A Message from the Grandmother Spirit After the Bombing of the World Trade Center and Pentagon* (2001), and *We Are the Ones We Have*

Been Waiting For (2006). Walker also wrote juvenile fiction and critical essays on such female writers as Flannery O'Connor and Zora Neale Hurston, and she cofounded a short-lived press in 1984.

African American men whose work gained attention during the latter decades of the 20th century included Ishmael Reed, whose wild comic techniques resembled Ellison's; James Alan McPherson, a subtle short-story writer in the mold of Ellison and Baldwin; Charles Johnson, whose novels, such as *The Oxherding Tale* (1982) and *The Middle Passage* (1990), showed a masterful historical imagination; Randall Kenan, a gay writer with a strong folk imagination whose style also descended from both Ellison and Baldwin; and Colson Whitehead, who used experimental techniques and folk traditions in *The Intuitionist* (1999) and *John Henry Days* (2001).

NEW FICTIONAL MODES

The horrors of World War II, the Cold War and the atomic bomb, the bizarre feast of consumer culture, and the cultural clashes of the 1960s prompted many writers to argue that reality had grown inaccessible, undermining the traditional social role of fiction. Writers of novels and short stories therefore were under unprecedented pressure to discover, or invent, new and viable kinds of fiction. One response was the postmodern novel of William Gaddis, John Barth, John Hawkes, Donald Barthelme, Thomas Pynchon, Robert Coover, Paul Auster, and Don DeLillo— technically sophisticated and highly self-conscious about the construction of fiction and the fictive nature of "reality" itself. These writers dealt with themes such as imposture and paranoia in novels that drew attention to themselves as artifacts and often used realistic techniques ironically. Other responses involved a heightening of realism by means of intensifying violence, amassing documentation, or resorting to fantasy. A brief discussion of writers as different as Norman Mailer and Joyce Carol Oates may serve to illustrate these new directions.

NORMAN MAILER

(b. Jan. 31, 1923, Long Branch, N.J.,—d. Nov. 10, 2007, New York, N.Y.)

Norman Mailer was a novelist and journalist best known for using "new journalism," combining the imaginative subjectivity of literature with the more objective qualities of journalism. Both Mailer's fiction and nonfiction radically critiqued the totalitarianism he believed inherent in the centralized power structure of 20th- and 21st-century America.

Born in 1923, Mailer grew up in Brooklyn and graduated from Harvard University in 1943 with a degree in aeronautical engineering. The following year he was drafted into the army, and he served in the Pacific until 1946. While he was enrolled at the Sorbonne, in Paris, he wrote the social protest novel *The Naked and the Dead* (1948), which was hailed immediately as one of the finest American novels to come out of World War II.

Mailer's success at age 25 aroused the expectation that he would develop from a war novelist into the leading literary figure of the postwar generation. But Mailer's search for themes and forms to give meaningful expression to what he saw as the problems of his time committed him to exploratory works that had little general appeal. His next novels, *Barbary Shore* (1951) and *The Deer Park* (1955), were greeted with critical hostility and mixed reviews, respectively. His next important work was a long essay, "The White Negro" (1957), a sympathetic study of a marginal social type—the "hipster."

In 1959, when Mailer was generally dismissed as a one-book author, he made a bid for attention with the book *Advertisements for Myself,* a collection of unfinished stories, parts of novels, essays, reviews, notebook entries, or ideas for fiction. The miscellany's naked self-revelation won the admiration of a younger generation seeking alternative styles of life and art. Mailer's subsequent novels, although not critical successes, were widely read as guides to life. *An American Dream* (1965) is about a man who murders his wife, and *Why Are We in Vietnam?* (1967) is about a young man on an Alaskan hunting trip.

A controversial figure whose egotism and belligerence often antagonized both critics and readers, Mailer did not command the same respect for his fiction that he received for his journalism, which conveyed actual events with the subjective richness and imaginative complexity of a novel. *The Armies of the Night* (1968), for example, was based on the Washington peace demonstrations of October 1967, during which Mailer was jailed and fined for an act of civil disobedience. It won a Pulitzer Prize and a National Book Award. A similar treatment was given the Republican and Democratic presidential conventions in *Miami and the Siege of Chicago* (1968) and the Moon exploration in *Of a Fire on the Moon* (1970).

Between publications, in 1969 Mailer ran unsuccessfully for mayor of New York City. Among his other works are his essay collections *The Presidential Papers* (1963) and *Cannibals and Christians* (1966); *The Executioner's Song* (1979), a Pulitzer Prize–winning novel based on the life of convicted murderer Gary Gilmore; *Ancient Evenings* (1983), a novel set in ancient Egypt, the first volume of an uncompleted trilogy; *Tough Guys Don't Dance* (1984), a contemporary mystery thriller; and the substantial *Harlot's Ghost* (1991), a novel focusing on the Central Intelligence Agency. In 1995 Mailer published *Oswald's Tale*, an exhaustive nonfictional portrayal of U.S. Pres. John F. Kennedy's assassin. Mailer's final two novels intertwined religion and historical figures: *The Gospel According to the Son* (1997) is a first-person "memoir" purportedly written by Jesus Christ, and *The Castle in the Forest* (2007), narrated by a devil, tells the story of Adolf Hitler's boyhood.

In 2003 Mailer published two works of nonfiction: *The Spooky Art*, his reflections on writing, and an essay questioning the Iraq War, *Why Are We at War?*

On God (2007) records conversations about religion between Mailer and the scholar Michael Lennon. Mailer died in New York City in 2007.

JOYCE CAROL OATES
(b. June 16, 1938, Lockport, New York)

The American novelist, short-story writer, and essayist Joyce Carol Oates is noted for her vast literary output in a variety of styles and genres. Particularly effective are her depictions of violence and evil in modern society.

Oates was born in New York state in 1938, the daughter of a tool-and-die designer. She studied English at Syracuse University (B.A., 1960) and the University of Wisconsin (M.A., 1961). She taught English at Michigan's University of Detroit from 1961 to 1967, and at the University of Windsor, in Ontario, Can., from 1967 to 1978. From 1978 she taught at Princeton University. In 1961 she married Raymond J. Smith, a fellow English student who also became a professor and an editor. Together they published the literary magazine, the *Ontario Review*.

Early in her career Oates contributed short stories to many magazines and reviews, including the *Prairie Schooner*, *Literary Review*, *Southwest Review*, and *Epoch*, and in 1963 published her first collection of short stories, *By the North Gate*. Her first novel, *With Shuddering Fall*, appeared in 1964 and was followed by a second collection, *Upon the Sweeping Flood* (1965). She wrote prolifically thereafter, averaging about two books per year.

Her notable fiction works include *A Garden of Earthly Delights* (1967), *them* (1969; winner of a National Book Award), *Do with Me What You Will* (1973), *Black Water* (1992), *Foxfire: Confessions of a Girl Gang* (1993), *Zombie* (1995), *We Were the Mulvaneys* (1996), *Broke Heart Blues* (1999), *The Falls* (2004), and *My Sister, My Love: The Intimate Story of Skyler Rampike* (2008). In 2001 she published the short-story collection *Faithless: Tales of Transgression*, "richly various" tales of sin. An extensive and mainly retrospective volume of her stories, *High Lonesome: New & Selected Stories, 1966–2006*, was published in 2006. The story collection *Wild Nights!: Stories About the Last Days of Poe, Dickinson, Twain, James, and Hemingway* (2008) featured fictionalized accounts of the final days of various iconic American writers. Oates also wrote mysteries (under the pseudonyms Rosamond Smith and Lauren Kelly), plays, essays, poetry, and literary criticism. Essays, reviews, and other prose pieces are included in *Where I've Been, and Where I'm Going* (1999).

Oates's novels encompass a variety of historical settings and literary genres. She typically portrays American individuals whose intensely experienced and obsessive lives end in bloodshed and self-destruction owing to larger forces beyond their control. Her books blend a realistic treatment of everyday life with horrific and even sensational depictions of violence. While Mailer and Oates refused to surrender the novel's gift for capturing reality, both were compelled to search out new fictional modes to tap that power.

The surge of feminism in the 1970s gave impetus to many new women writers, such as Erica Jong, author of the sexy and funny *Fear of Flying* (1974), and Rita Mae

Brown, who explored lesbian life in *Rubyfruit Jungle* (1973). Other significant works of fiction by women in the 1970s included Ann Beattie's account of the post-1960s generation in *Chilly Scenes of Winter* (1976) and many short stories, Gail Godwin's highly civilized *The Odd Woman* (1974), Mary Gordon's portraits of Irish Catholic life in *Final Payments* (1978), and the many social comedies of Alison Lurie and Anne Tyler.

THE INFLUENCE OF RAYMOND CARVER

Perhaps the most influential American fiction writer to emerge in the 1970s was Raymond Carver. He was another realist who dealt with blue-collar life, usually in the Pacific Northwest, in powerful collections of stories such as *What We Talk About When We Talk About Love* (1981) and *Cathedral* (1983). His self-destructive characters were life's losers, and his style, influenced by Hemingway and Samuel Beckett, was spare and flat but powerfully suggestive.

Raymond Carver etched a niche for his terse fiction, which contains depictions of struggling, working-class characters. ANP/Newscom

Carver was born in 1938 in rural Oregon and was the son of a sawmill worker. He married a year after finishing high school and supported his wife and two children by working as a janitor, gas station attendant, and delivery man. He became seriously interested in a writing career after taking a creative writing course at Chico State College (now California State University, Chico) in 1958. His short stories began to appear in magazines while he studied at Humboldt State College (now Humboldt State University) in Arcata, Calif. (B.A., 1963). Carver's first success as a writer came in 1967 with the story "Will You Please Be Quiet, Please?" He began writing full-time after losing his job as a textbook editor in 1970, and the highly successful short-story collection *Will You Please Be Quiet, Please?* (1976) established his reputation.

Carver began drinking heavily in 1967 and was repeatedly hospitalized for alcoholism in the 1970s, while continuing to turn out short stories. After conquering his drinking problem in the late 1970s, he taught for several years at the University of Texas at El Paso and at Syracuse University, and in 1983 he won a literary award whose generous annual stipend freed him to again concentrate on his writing full time. His later short-story collections were *What We Talk About When We Talk About Love* (1981), *Cathedral* (1984), and *Where I'm Calling From* (1988). His short stories were what made his critical reputation, but he was also an accomplished poet in the realist tradition of Robert Frost. Carver's poetry collections include *At Night the Salmon Move* (1976), *Where Water Comes Together with Other Water* (1985), and *Ultramarine* (1986). He died of lung cancer at age 50.

In his short stories Carver chronicled the everyday lives and problems of the working poor in the Pacific Northwest. His blue-collar characters are crushed by broken marriages, financial problems, and failed careers, but they are often unable to understand or even articulate their own anguish. Carver's stripped-down, minimalist prose style is remarkable for its honesty and power. He is credited with helping revitalize the genre of the English-language short story in the late 20th century.

However, controversy arose over the nature of Carver's writing—and even his lasting literary reputation—in the early 21st century. It was revealed that his long-time editor, Gordon Lish, had drastically changed many of Carver's early stories. Although Lish's significant involvement in Carver's writing had long been suspected, the extent of his editing became public knowledge when, in 2007, Carver's widow, the poet Tess Gallagher, announced that she was seeking to publish the original versions of the stories in *What We Talk About When We Talk About Love* (which appeared in the U.K. as *Beginners* in 2009). Lish was shown to have changed characters' names, cut the length of many stories (more than 75 percent of the text in two cases), and altered the endings of some stories. However, most of Carver's famously terse sentences were his own, as was the hallmark bleak, working-class milieu of the short stories.

Carver's style was imitated, often badly, by minimalists such as Frederick Barthelme, Mary Robison, and Amy Hempel. More talented writers whose novels reflected the influence of Carver in their evocation of the downbeat world of the blue-collar male included Richard Ford (*Rock Springs* [1987]), Russell Banks (*Continental Drift* [1984] and *Affliction* [1989]), and Tobias Wolff (*The Barracks Thief* [1984] and *This Boy's Life* [1989]).

Another strong male-oriented writer in a realist mode who emerged from the 1960s counterculture was Robert Stone. His *Dog Soldiers* (1974) was a grimly downbeat portrayal of the drugs-and-Vietnam generation, and *A Flag for Sunrise* (1981) was a bleak, Conradian political novel set in Central America. Stone focused more on the spiritual malaise of his characters than on their ordinary lives. He wrote a lean, furious Hollywood novel in *Children of Light*

(1986) and captured some of the feverish, apocalyptic atmosphere of the Holy Land in *Damascus Gate* (1998).

In leisurely, good-humoured, minutely detailed novels, Richard Russo dealt with blue-collar losers living in decaying Northeastern towns in *The Risk Pool* (1988), *Nobody's Fool* (1993), and *Empire Falls* (2001), but he also published a satiric novel about academia, *Straight Man* (1997).

Some women writers were especially impressive in dealing with male characters, including E. Annie Proulx in *The Shipping News* (1993) and *Close Range: Wyoming Stories* (1999) and Andrea Barrett in *Ship Fever* (1996). Others focused on relationships between women, including Mary Gaitskill in her witty satiric novel *Two Girls, Fat and Thin* (1991), written under the influences of Nabokov and Mary McCarthy. Lorrie Moore published rich, idiosyncratic stories as densely textured as novels. Deborah Eisenberg, Amy Bloom, Antonya Nelson, and Thom Jones also helped make the last years of the 20th century a fertile period for short fiction.

E. Annie Proulx

(b. Aug. 22, 1935, Norwich, Conn.)

E. Annie Proulx is known for her darkly comic yet sad fiction, peopled with quirky, memorable individuals and unconventional families. Proulx traveled widely, extensively researching physical backgrounds and locales. She frequently used regional speech patterns, surprising and scathing language, and unusual plot twists in her novels and short stories about disintegrating families who maintain attachments to the land.

Educated at the University of Vermont (B.A., 1969) and Sir George Williams University, Montreal, Can. (M.A., 1973), Edna Annie Proulx settled in northern Vermont and later in Wyoming. She lived close to the land, about which she wrote frequently in freelance articles for such magazines as *Gourmet*.

After publication of her first short-story collection, *Heart Songs, and Other Stories* (1988), Proulx turned to writing novels, which better accommodated her dense plots and complex characterizations. *Postcards* (1992), her first novel, uses the device of picture postcards mailed from the road over 40 years' time to illustrate changes in American life. The postcards are sent by Loyal Blood, who accidentally kills his girlfriend and abandons his family and their meager Vermont farm, escaping to a life of picaresque adventures.

In *The Shipping News* (1993; film 2001), the protagonist Quoyle and his family, consisting of two young daughters and his aunt, leave the United States and settle in Newfoundland, Can., after the accidental death of his unfaithful wife. *The Shipping News* was awarded both a Pulitzer Prize and a National Book Award. Proulx's next novel was *Accordion Crimes* (1996), which examines the immigrant experience by tracing the life of an Old World accordion in the United States.

Close Range: Wyoming Stories (1999) is a collection of stories set in the harsh landscapes of rural Wyoming. It includes *Brokeback Mountain*, the story of two ranch hands, Jack Twist and Ennis del Mar, whose friendship becomes a sexual relationship during a summer spent tending sheep in the 1960s. Afterward they pursue the traditional heterosexual lives expected of them but experience a lifetime of longing for each other. Originally published in the *New Yorker* magazine in 1997, Proulx's story was adapted as the film *Brokeback Mountain* (2005), directed by Ang Lee with a screenplay by Larry McMurtry and Diana Ossana. In 2002 Proulx published the novel *That Old Ace in the Hole* about a man who scouts the Texas Panhandle for land to be acquired by a major corporation. *Bad Dirt: Wyoming Stories 2* (2004) and *Fine Just the Way It Is: Wyoming Stories 3* (2008) are collections of short stories.

MULTICULTURAL WRITING

The dramatic loosening of immigration restrictions in the mid-1960s set the stage for the rich multicultural writing of the last quarter of the 20th century. New Jewish voices were heard in the fiction of E.L. Doctorow, noted for his mingling of the historical with the fictional in novels such as *Ragtime* (1975) and *The Waterworks* (1994) and in the work of Cynthia Ozick, whose best story, *Envy; or Yiddish in America* (1969), has characters modeled on leading figures in Yiddish literature. Her story "The Shawl" (1980) concerns the murder of a baby in a Nazi concentration camp. David Leavitt introduced homosexual themes into his portrayal of middle-class life in *Family Dancing* (1984). At the turn of the 21st century, younger Jewish writers from the former Soviet Union such as Gary Shteyngart and Lara Vapnyar dealt impressively with the experience of immigrants in the United States.

Novels such as N. Scott Momaday's *House Made of Dawn*, which won the Pulitzer Prize in 1969; James Welch's *Winter in the Blood* (1974) and *Fools Crow* (1986); Leslie Marmon Silko's *Ceremony* (1977); and Louise Erdrich's *Love Medicine* (1984), *The Beet Queen* (1986), and *The Antelope Wife* (1998) were powerful and ambiguous explorations of Native American history and identity. Mexican Americans were represented by works such as Rudolfo A. Anaya's *Bless Me, Ultima* (1972); Richard Rodriguez's autobiographical *Hunger of Memory* (1981); and Sandra Cisneros's *The House on Mango Street* (1983) and her collection *Woman Hollering Creek, and Other Stories* (1991).

Some of the best immigrant writers, while thoroughly assimilated, nonetheless had a subtle understanding of both the old and the new culture. These included the Cuban American writers Oscar Hijuelos (*The Mambo Kings Play Songs of Love* [1989]) and Cristina Garcia (*Dreaming in Cuban* [1992] and *The Agüero Sisters* [1997]); the Antigua-born Jamaica Kincaid, author of *Annie John* (1984), *Lucy* (1990), and an AIDS memoir, *My Brother* (1997); the Dominican-born Junot Díaz, who won acclaim for *Drown* (1996), a collection of stories, and whose novel *The Brief*

Wondrous Life of Oscar Wao (2007) won a Pulitzer Prize; and the Bosnian immigrant Aleksandar Hemon, who wrote *The Question of Bruno* (2000) and *Nowhere Man* (2002). Chinese Americans found an extraordinary voice in Maxine Hong Kingston's *The Woman Warrior* (1976) and *China Men* (1980), which blended old Chinese lore with fascinating family history. Her first novel, *Tripmaster Monkey: His Fake Book* (1989), was set in the bohemian world of the San Francisco Bay area during the 1960s. Other important Asian American writers included Gish Jen, whose *Typical American* (1991) dealt with immigrant striving and frustration; the Korean American Chang-rae Lee, who focused on family life, political awakening, and generational differences in *Native Speaker* (1995) and *A Gesture Life* (1999); and Ha Jin, whose *Waiting* (1999, National Book Award), set in rural China during and after the Cultural Revolution, was a powerful tale of timidity, repression, and botched love, contrasting the mores of the old China and the new. Bharati Mukherjee beautifully explored contrasting lives in India and North America in *The Middleman and Other Stories* (1988), *Jasmine* (1989), and *Desirable Daughters* (2002). Many multicultural works were merely representative of their cultural milieu, but books such as these made remarkable contributions to a changing American literature.

During the 1990s some of the best energies of fiction writers went into autobiography, in works such as Mary Karr's *The Liar's Club* (1995), about growing up in a loving but dysfunctional family on the Texas Gulf Coast; Frank McCourt's *Angela's Ashes* (1996), a vivid portrayal of a Dickensian childhood amid the grinding conditions of Irish slum life; Anne Roiphe's bittersweet recollections of her rich but coldhearted parents and her brother's death from AIDS in *1185 Park Avenue* (1999); and Dave Eggers's *A Heartbreaking Work of Staggering Genius* (2000), a painful but comic tour de force, half tongue-in-cheek, about a young man raising his brother after the death of their parents.

The memoir vogue did not prevent writers from publishing huge, ambitious novels, including David Foster Wallace's *Infinite Jest* (1996), an encyclopaedic mixture of arcane lore, social fiction, and postmodern irony; Jonathan Franzen's *The Corrections* (2001, National Book Award), an affecting, scathingly satiric family portrait; and Don DeLillo's *Underworld* (1997), a brooding, resonant, oblique account of the Cold War era as seen through the eyes of both fictional characters and historical figures. All three novels testify to a belated convergence of Social Realism and Pynchonesque invention. Pynchon himself returned to form with a sprawling, picaresque historical novel, *Mason & Dixon* (1997), about two famous 18th-century surveyors who explored and mapped the American colonies.

CHAPTER 2

OTHER SIGNIFICANT NOVELISTS AND SHORT-STORY WRITERS OF THE POSTWAR ERA

As the uniformity of mass media was fractured by post–World War II technological advances, a number of new literary genres came to prominence to meet the increasingly diverse interests of the reading public. Although much writing in the popular "pulp" genres, such as science fiction and hard-boiled detective novels, was not particularly noteworthy, there were a great many standout authors in these supposedly "less-serious" styles of fiction.

This is not to say that writing in traditional literary genres disappeared after World War II. From historical novels to westerns, authors working in many long-established genres produced landmark works at this time that compare favourably with established classics. In addition, writers whose experimental work cannot be categorized into genres also thrived during this era.

NELSON ALGREN

(b. March 28, 1909, Detroit, Mich.—d. May 9, 1981, Sag Harbor, N.Y.)

Nelson Algren's novels of the poor are lifted from routine naturalism by his vision of their pride, humour, and unquenchable yearnings. He also catches with poetic skill the mood of the city's underside: its jukebox pounding, stench, and neon glare.

The son of a machinist, Algren grew up in Chicago, where his parents moved when he was three years old. He worked his way through the University of Illinois, graduating in journalism in the depth of the Great Depression. Sometime after graduating, he adopted a simplified spelling of the original name, Ahlgren, of his Swedish grandfather, who had converted to Judaism and taken the name Abraham. He went on the road as a door-to-door salesman and migratory worker in the South and Southwest, then returned to Chicago, where he was employed briefly by a WPA (Works Progress Administration) writers' project and a venereal-disease control unit of the Board of Health. In this period, too, he edited with the proletarian novelist Jack Conroy the *New Anvil*, a magazine dedicated to the publication of experimental and leftist writing.

Algren's first novel, *Somebody in Boots* (1935), relates the Depression-era driftings of a young poor-white Texan who ends up among the down-and-outs of Chicago. *Never Come Morning* (1942) tells of a Polish petty criminal who dreams of escaping from his squalid Northwest Side Chicago environment by becoming a prizefighter. Before the appearance of Algren's next book—the short-story collection *The Neon Wilderness* (1947), which contains some of his best writing—he served as a U.S. Army medical corpsman during World War II.

In 1947 Algren met the French writer and feminist Simone de Beauvoir. The two began a transatlantic relationship that lasted 17 years. De Beauvoir dedicated her novel *Les Mandarins* (1954, *The Mandarins*) to him, limning him in the character Lewis Brogan.

Algren's first popular success was *The Man with the Golden Arm* (1949; film 1956), which won the first National Book Award for fiction. Its hero is Frankie Machine, whose golden arm as a poker dealer is threatened by shakiness connected with his drug addiction. In *A Walk on the Wild Side* (1956; film 1962) Algren returned to the 1930s in a picaresque novel of New Orleans bohemian life. After 1959 he abandoned novel writing (although he continued to publish short stories) and considered himself a journalist. He completed his last novel, *The Devil's Stocking*, in 1979, but it was rejected by many publishers and posthumously published in 1983.

Algren's nonfiction includes the prose poem *Chicago, City on the Make* (1951) as well as sketches collected as *Who Lost an American?* (1963) and *Notes from a Sea Diary: Hemingway All the Way* (1965). Algren was elected to the American Academy and Institute of Arts and Letters three months before he died.

ISAAC ASIMOV

(b. Jan. 2, 1920, Petrovichi, Russia—d. April 6, 1992, New York, N.Y.)

Author and biochemist Isaac Asimov was a highly successful and prolific writer of science fiction and science books for the layperson. He published about 500 volumes.

Asimov was brought to the United States at age three. He grew up in Brooklyn, N.Y., graduating from Columbia University in 1939 and taking a Ph.D. there in 1948. He then joined the faculty of Boston University, with which he remained associated thereafter.

Asimov began contributing stories to science fiction magazines in 1939 and in 1950 published his first book, *Pebble in the Sky*. His trilogy of novels, *Foundation, Foundation and Empire*, and *Second Foundation* (1951–53), which recounts the collapse and rebirth of a vast interstellar empire in the universe of the future, is his most famous work of science fiction. In the short-story collection *I, Robot* (1950; film 2004), he developed a set of ethics for robots and intelligent machines that greatly influenced other writers' treatment of the subject. His other novels and collections of stories included *The Stars, like Dust* (1951), *The Currents of Space* (1952), *The Caves of Steel* (1954), *The Naked Sun* (1957), *Earth Is Room Enough* (1957), *Foundation's Edge* (1982), and *The Robots of Dawn* (1983). His "Nightfall" (1941) is thought by many to be the finest science fiction short story ever written. Among Asimov's books on various topics in science, written with lucidity and humour, are *The Chemicals of Life* (1954), *Inside the Atom* (1956), *The World of Nitrogen* (1958), *Life and Energy* (1962), *The Human Brain* (1964), *The Neutrino* (1966), *Science, Numbers, and I* (1968), *Our World in Space* (1974), and *Views of the Universe* (1981). He also published two volumes of autobiography.

RUSSELL BANKS

(b. March 28, 1940, Newton, Mass.)

The American novelist Russell Banks is known for his portrayals of the interior lives of characters at odds with economic and social forces.

Banks was educated at Colgate University (Hamilton, N.Y.) and the University of North Carolina. From 1966 he was associated with Lillabulero Press, initially as editor and publisher. The press issued his first book of poems, *Waiting to Freeze*, in 1969. Other early works include the poetry collection *Snow: Meditations of a Cautious Man in Winter* (1974); Banks's first novel, *Family Life* (1975); and a collection of stories entitled *The New World* (1978). His novel *Hamilton Stark* (1978) is notable for its vividly rendered hardscrabble New Hampshire setting. The story collection *Trailerpark* (1981) explores the same locale. An experimental novel, *The Relation of My Imprisonment* (1984), set in 17th-century New England, was regarded by most reviewers as conceptually and stylistically flawed. Banks's interest in the Caribbean, which led to his residence in Jamaica for an interval, shaped two of his novels, *The Book of Jamaica* (1980) and *Continental Drift* (1985), the latter being generally considered his best work. His subsequent novels include *Affliction* (1989; film 1997), *The Sweet Hereafter* (1991; film 1997), and *Rule of the Bone* (1995). The last of these, with its clear-sighted 14-year-old protagonist, is reminiscent of J.D. Salinger's *The Catcher in the Rye*.

In 1998 Banks published *Cloudsplitter*, the fictional response of John Brown's unhappy son to the actions of his father and the racism that precipitated them, and in 2000 he published a collection of stories titled *The Angel on the Roof*. Other novels include *The Darling* (2005), a tragic narrative of a politically radical American woman in war-torn Liberia, and *The Reserve* (2008), a combined love story and murder mystery. *Dreaming Up America* (2008) is a nonfiction work scrutinizing the history of destructive and constructive policies pursued by the United States.

OCTAVIA E. BUTLER

(b. June 22, 1947, Pasadena, Calif.—d. February 24, 2006, Seattle, Wash.)

Author Octavia Estelle Butler is noted chiefly for her science fiction novels about future societies and superhuman powers. They are noteworthy for their unique synthesis of science fiction, mysticism, mythology, and African American spiritualism.

Butler was educated at Pasadena City College (A.A., 1968), California State University, and the University of

California at Los Angeles. Encouraged by Harlan Ellison, she began her writing career in 1970. The first of her novels, *Patternmaster* (1976), was the beginning of her five-volume Patternist series about an elite group of mentally linked telepaths ruled by Doro, a 4,000-year-old immortal African. Other novels in the series are *Mind of My Mind* (1977), *Survivor* (1978), *Wild Seed* (1980), and *Clay's Ark* (1984).

In *Kindred* (1979) a contemporary black woman is sent back in time to a pre–Civil War plantation, becomes a slave, and rescues her white, slave-owning ancestor. Her later novels include the Xenogenesis trilogy—*Dawn: Xenogenesis* (1987), *Adulthood Rites* (1988), and *Imago* (1989)—and *The Parable of the Sower* (1993), *The Parable of the Talents* (1998), and *Fledgling* (2005). Butler's short story "Speech Sounds" won a Hugo Award in 1984, and her story "Bloodchild," about human male slaves who incubate their alien masters' eggs, won both Hugo and Nebula awards. Her collection *Bloodchild and Other Stories* was published in 1995. That same year Butler became the first science fiction writer to be awarded a MacArthur Foundation fellowship, and in 2000 she received a PEN Award for lifetime achievement.

SANDRA CISNEROS

(b. December 20, 1954, Chicago, Ill.)

The short-story writer and poet Sandra Cisneros is best known for her groundbreaking evocation of Mexican American life in Chicago.

After graduating from Chicago's Loyola University (B.A., 1976), Cisneros attended the University of Iowa Writers' Workshop (M.F.A., 1978). There she developed what was to be the theme of most of her writing, her unique experiences as a Hispanic woman in a largely alien culture.

Cisneros's first book was *Bad Boys* (1980), a volume of poetry. She gained international attention with her first book of fiction, *The House on Mango Street* (1983), written in a defiant youthful voice that reflected her own memories of a girlhood spent trying to be a creative writer in an antagonistic environment. More poetry—including *The Rodrigo Poems* (1985), *My Wicked, Wicked Ways* (1987), and *Loose Woman* (1994)—followed. Her collection of short stories, *Woman Hollering Creek and Other Stories* (1991), contains tales of beleaguered girls and women who nonetheless feel that they have power over their destinies. She returned to long fiction with *Caramelo; o, puro cuento* (2002), a semi-autobiographical work that echoes her own peripatetic childhood in a large family.

RAYMOND CHANDLER

(b. July 23, 1888, Chicago, Ill.—d. March 26, 1959, La Jolla, Calif.)

Raymond Chandler was an author of detective fiction and the creator of the private detective Philip Marlowe, whom he characterized as a poor but honest upholder of ideals in an opportunistic and sometimes brutal society in Los Angeles.

From 1896 to 1912 Chandler lived in England with his mother, a British subject of Irish birth. Although he was an American citizen and a resident of California when World War I began in 1914, he served in the Canadian army and then in the Royal Flying Corps (afterward the Royal Air Force). Having returned to California in 1919, he prospered as a petroleum company executive until the Great Depression of the 1930s, when he turned to writing for a living. His first published short story appeared in the "pulp" magazine *Black Mask* in 1933. From 1943 he was a Hollywood screenwriter. Among his best-known scripts were for the films *Double Indemnity* (1944), *The Blue Dahlia*

Raymond Chandler created the forthright detective Philip Marlowe, a character in striking contrast to the corrupt Los Angeles society that served as a backdrop for his stories. Ralph Crane/Time & Life Pictures/Getty Images

(1946), and *Strangers on a Train* (1951), the last written in collaboration with Czenzi Ormonde.

Chandler completed seven novels, all with Philip Marlowe as hero: *The Big Sleep* (1939), *Farewell, My Lovely*

(1940), *The High Window* (1942), *The Lady in the Lake* (1943), *The Little Sister* (1949), *The Long Goodbye* (1953), and *Playback* (1958). Among his numerous short-story collections are *Five Murderers* (1944) and *The Midnight Raymond Chandler* (1971). The most popular film versions of Chandler's work were *Murder, My Sweet* (1945; also distributed as *Farewell, My Lovely*), starring Dick Powell, and *The Big Sleep* (1946), starring Humphrey Bogart, both film noir classics.

Hard-Boiled Fiction

The novels of Raymond Chandler, which deal with corruption and racketeering in Southern California, are considered part of the hard-boiled genre of fiction. The term "hard-boiled fiction" refers to a tough, unsentimental style of American crime writing that, when it first gained prominence in the 1930s, brought a new tone of earthy realism or naturalism to the field of detective fiction. Hard-boiled fiction uses graphic sex and violence, vivid but often sordid urban backgrounds, and fast-paced, slangy dialogue.

Credit for the invention of the genre belongs to Dashiell Hammett (1894–1961), a former Pinkerton detective and contributor to the pulp magazines, whose first truly hard-boiled story, "Fly Paper," appeared in *Black Mask* magazine in 1929. Combining his own experiences with the realistic influence of writers such as Ernest Hemingway and John Dos Passos, Hammett created a definitively American type of detective fiction that was separate and distinct from the English mystery story usually set in a country house populated by cooks, butlers, and relatives, a pattern that had been slavishly followed by American writers for generations. The first of Hammett's detective novels was *Red Harvest* (1929). His masterpiece is generally believed to be *The Maltese Falcon* (1930), which introduced Sam Spade, his most famous sleuth. His most successful story, *The Thin Man* (1934), was the last of an extraordinary quintet of novels.

Hammett's innovations were incorporated in the hard-boiled melodramas of James M. Cain (1892–1977), particularly in

Humphrey Bogart (shown with Lauren Bacall) portrayed hard-boiled detective Philip Marlowe in the film adaptation of Chandler's novel The Big Sleep. *The gruff, hard-boiled detective was a mainstay in crime fiction of the era.* Warner Bros./Hulton Archive/Getty Images

such early works as *The Postman Always Rings Twice* (1934) and *Double Indemnity* (1936). In addition to Cain and Chandler, other important writers of the hard-boiled school are George Harmon Coxe (1901–84), author of such thrillers as *Murder with Pictures* (1935) and *Eye Witness* (1950), and W.R. Burnett (1899–1982), who wrote *Little Caesar* (1929) and *The Asphalt Jungle* (1949). Hard-boiled fiction ultimately degenerated into the extreme sensationalism and undisguised sadism of what *Ellery Queen's Mystery Magazine* called

the "guts-gore-and-gals-school," as found in the works of Mickey
Spillane, writer of such phenomenal best sellers as *I, the Jury* (1947).
The works of the hard-boiled school have been extensively
translated into films, often through successive versions tailored
to different generations of moviegoers.

ROBERT COOVER

(b. Feb. 4, 1932, Charles City, Iowa)

Robert Coover's avant-garde fiction, plays, poetry, and
essays are highlighted by their experimental forms and techniques that mix reality and illusion, frequently creating
otherworldly and surreal situations and effects.

Coover attended Southern Illinois University, Indiana
University (B.A., 1953), and the University of Chicago
(M.A., 1965). He taught at several universities, notably
Brown University in Providence, Rhode Island.

His first, and most conventional, novel, *The Origin of
the Brunists* (1966), tells of the rise and eventual disintegration of a religious cult. The protagonist of *The Universal
Baseball Association, Inc.* (1968) creates an imaginary baseball league, in which fictitious players take charge of their
own lives. Written in the voice of Richard Nixon and satirizing the national mood of the early 1950s, *The Public
Burning* (1976) is what Coover called a "factional account"
of the trial and execution of Julius and Ethel Rosenberg.
Among his other works are *Whatever Happened to Gloomy
Gus of the Chicago Bears?* (1987), *Pinocchio in Venice* (1991),
John's Wife (1996), *Ghost Town* (1998), and *The Adventures of
Lucky Pierre: Director's Cut* (2002), the tale of an idolized
pornographic-film actor who lives in a society of limitless
sexual extravagance.

Coover's short-story collection *Pricksongs & Descants*
(1969) was praised for its "verbal magic," and several of his

stories were adapted for theatrical performance, including "The Baby Sitter" (film 1995) and "Spanking the Maid." In 2002 he published *The Grand Hotels (of Joseph Cornell)*, a collection of 10 poetic vignettes derived from Joseph Cornell's assemblages. Coover explored children's literature through *Stepmother* (2004), an illustrated modern fairy tale for adults, and *A Child Again* (2005), a collection of grotesque retellings of childhood tales.

DON DELILLO

(b. Nov. 20, 1936, New York, N.Y.)

The novelist Don DeLillo is known for postmodernist works that portray the anomie of an America cosseted by material excess and stupefied by empty mass culture and politics.

After his graduation from Fordham University, New York City (1958), DeLillo worked for several years as a copywriter at an advertising agency. DeLillo's first novel, *Americana* (1971), is the story of a network television executive in search of the "real" America. It was followed by *End Zone* (1972) and *Great Jones Street* (1973). *Ratner's Star* (1976) attracted critical attention with its baroque comic sense and verbal facility.

Beginning with *Players* (1977), DeLillo's vision turned darker, and his characters became more willful in their destructiveness and ignorance. Critics found little to like in the novel's protagonists but much to admire in DeLillo's elliptical prose. The thrillers *Running Dog* (1978) and *The Names* (1982) followed. *White Noise* (1985), which won the American Book Award for fiction, tells of a professor of Hitler studies who is exposed to an "airborne toxic event." When he discovers that his wife is taking an experimental substance said to combat the fear of death, he vows to obtain the drug for himself at any cost. In *Libra* (1988), DeLillo presented a fictional portrayal of Lee Harvey

Oswald, the assassin of Pres. John F. Kennedy. *Mao II* (1991) opens with a mass wedding officiated by cult leader Sun Myung Moon. It tells the story of a reclusive writer who becomes enmeshed in a world of political violence.

DeLillo's later works of fiction include *Underworld* (1997), which provides a commentary on American history in the second half of the 20th century by tracing the journeys of a baseball, as well as *Cosmopolis* (2003), set largely in a billionaire's limousine as it moves across Manhattan, and *Falling Man* (2007), which tells the story of a survivor of the September 11 attacks in 2001.

PHILIP K. DICK

(b. Dec. 16, 1928, Chicago, Ill.—d. March 2, 1982, Santa Ana, Calif.)

Philip K. Dick was a science fiction writer whose novels and short stories often depict the psychological struggles of characters trapped in illusory environments.

Philip Kindred Dick worked briefly in radio before studying at the University of California, Berkeley, for one year. The publication of his first story, "Beyond Lies the Wub," in 1952 launched his full-time writing career, which was marked by extraordinary productivity, as he oftentimes completed a new work, usually a short story or a novella, every two weeks for printing in pulp paperback collections. He published his first novel, *Solar Lottery*, in 1955. Early in Dick's work the theme emerged that would remain his central preoccupation—that of a reality at variance with what it appeared or was intended to be. In such novels as *Time out of Joint* (1959), *The Man in the High Castle* (1962; Hugo Award winner), and *The Three Stigmata of Palmer Eldritch* (1965), the protagonists must determine their own orientation in an "alternate world." Beginning with *The Simulacra* (1964) and culminating in *Do Androids*

91

Dream of Electric Sheep? (1968; adapted for film as *Blade Runner*, 1982), the illusion centres on artificial creatures at large and grappling with what is authentic in a real world of the future.

After years of drug abuse and mental illness, Dick died impoverished and with little literary reputation outside of science fiction circles. By the 21st century, however, he was widely regarded as a master of imaginitve, paranoid fiction in the vein of Franz Kafka and Thomas Pynchon. Although his works can definitively be categorized as science fiction, Dick was notable for focusing not on the trappings of futuristic technology, as many writers in the genre do, but on the discomfiting effects that these radically different—and often dystopian—surroundings have on the characters.

Among Dick's numerous story collections are *A Handful of Darkness* (1955), *The Variable Man and Other Stories* (1957), *The Preserving Machine* (1969), and the posthumously published *I Hope I Shall Arrive Soon* (1985). Several of his short stories and novels have been adapted for film, including *We Can Remember It for You Wholesale* (filmed as *Total Recall*, 1990), *Second Variety* (filmed as *Screamers*, 1995), *The Minority Report* (filmed as *Minority Report*, 2002), and *A Scanner Darkly* (1977; film 2006).

E.L. DOCTOROW

(b. Jan. 6, 1931, New York, N.Y.)

American novelist E.L. Doctorow is known for his skillful manipulation of traditional genres.

Edgar Lawrence Doctorow graduated from Kenyon College (B.A., 1952) and then studied drama and directing for a year at Columbia University. He worked for a time as a script reader for Columbia Pictures in New York City. In 1959 he joined the editorial staff of the New American

Library, leaving that post five years later to become editor in chief at Dial Press. He subsequently taught at several colleges and universities, including Sarah Lawrence College from 1971 to 1978. He was a visiting senior fellow at Princeton University in 1980–81 and the following year became Glucksman Professor of English and American Letters at New York University.

Doctorow was noted for the facility with which he appropriated genre conceits to illuminate the historical periods in which he set his novels. His first novel, *Welcome to Hard Times* (1960; film 1967), is a philosophical turn on the western genre. In his next book, *Big As Life* (1966), he used science fiction to explore the human response to crisis. Doctorow's proclivity for harvesting characters from history first became apparent in *The Book of Daniel* (1971; film 1983), a fictionalized treatment of the execution of Julius and Ethel Rosenberg for espionage in 1953. In *Ragtime* (1975; film 1981), historical figures share the spotlight with characters emblematic of the shifting social dynamics of early 20th-century America.

Doctorow then turned to the milieu of the Great Depression and its aftermath in the novels *Loon Lake* (1980), *World's Fair* (1985), and *Billy Bathgate* (1989; film 1991). *The Waterworks* (1994) concerns life in 19th-century New York. *City of God* (2000), consisting of what are ostensibly the journal entries of a writer, splinters into several different narratives, including a detective story and a Holocaust narrative. *The March* (2005) follows a fictionalized version of the Union general William Tecumseh Sherman on his infamously destructive trek through Georgia, aimed at weakening the Confederate economy, during the American Civil War. Doctorow trained his sights on historical figures of less eminence in *Homer and Langley* (2009), a mythologization of the lives of the Collyer brothers, a pair of reclusive eccentrics whose death in 1947 revealed a nightmarish repository of curiosities and garbage in their Harlem, New York City, brownstone.

Doctorow's essays were collected in several volumes, including *Reporting the Universe* (2003) and *Creationists: Selected Essays, 1993–2006* (2006), which contrasts the creative process as it manifests in literature and in science. Additionally, Doctorow wrote the play *Drinks Before Dinner* (1979) and published the short-story collections *Lives of the Poets* (1984) and *Sweet Land Stories* (2004).

RICHARD FORD

(b. Feb. 16, 1944, Jackson, Miss.)

In his novels and short stories, Richard Ford examined the lives of lonely and damaged people.

Ford attended Michigan State University (B.A., 1966), Washington University Law School, and the University of California, Irvine (M.A., 1970), and he subsequently taught at several American colleges and universities. He worked as a sportswriter during the 1980s.

Ford's first novel, *A Piece of My Heart* (1976), is set on an island in the southern Mississippi River and contrasts an intellectual with an impulsive man in an atmosphere of menace and violence. Critics noted the influence of William Faulkner in this novel. *The Ultimate Good Luck* (1981) presents an American in Mexico who is drawn reluctantly into violence and murder as he tries to get his girlfriend's brother out of jail. Frank Bascombe, the protagonist of *The Sportswriter* (1986), is an alienated, middle-aged sportswriter reflecting on his life. Bascombe returns in the Pulitzer Prize–winning *Independence Day* (1995), in which he is divorced and leading an empty life until he spends an emotional and spiritual Fourth of July weekend with his son. Completing the Bascombe trilogy is *The Lay of the*

Land (2006), in which Bascombe, now a suburban
real estate agent, faces aging, further marital problems,
estrangement from his adult children, and cancer.

Wildlife (1990) depicts a teenager in Montana who
witnesses the breakup of his parents' marriage. *Rock
Springs* (1987), *Women with Men* (1997), and *A Multitude of
Sins* (2001) are collections of short stories, the last about
the complications of love and infidelity. Ford also coedited *The Best American Short Stories of 1990* (1990) and
edited *The Granta Book of the American Short Story* (1991)
and *The New Granta Book of the American Short Story* (2007).

WILLIAM GADDIS

(b. Dec. 29, 1922, New York, N.Y.—d. Dec. 16, 1998, East
Hampton, N.Y.)

An American novelist of complex, satiric works, William
Gaddis is considered one of the best of the post–World
War II Modernist writers.

After incomplete studies at Harvard University (1941–
45), Gaddis worked as a fact-checker for the *New Yorker*
magazine for two years and then traveled widely in Central
America and Europe, holding a variety of jobs. He first
gained note as an author with the publication of his controversial novel *The Recognitions* (1955). This book, rich in
language and imagery, began as a parody of Faust but
developed into a multileveled examination of spiritual
bankruptcy that alternately was considered a brilliant
masterpiece and incomprehensibly excessive. It became
an underground classic, but, discouraged by the harsh
critical reception of his book, Gaddis worked as a freelance writer for various corporations and published
nothing for 20 years. His second novel, *JR* (1975), uses long
stretches of cacophonous dialogue to depict what he
viewed as the greed, hypocrisy, and banality of the world

of American business. Gaddis's third novel, *Carpenter's Gothic* (1985), is even more pessimistic in its depiction of moral chaos in modern America. The law, lawyers, and especially the litigiousness rampant in contemporary American society are examined in *A Frolic of His Own* (1994). Gaddis's last work of fiction, *Agapē Agape*, a rambling first-person narrative of a dying man obsessed with the history of the player piano, was published posthumously in 2002, as was the collection *The Rush for Second Place: Essays and Occasional Writings*.

Gaddis's fiction shows the influence of the writings of James Joyce and in turn influenced the work of Thomas Pynchon, containing long dialogues and monologues connected by a minimal plotline and structured with scant punctuation. His books belong to a style of literature characterized by the absence of distinctive incidents and by the pervasive use of black humour in dealing with a chaotic mass of associations. They create a radical way of viewing the world by which the reader can reassess his own situation.

WILLIAM GIBSON

(b. March 17, 1948, Conway, S.C.)

The American Canadian science fiction writer William Gibson is known as the leader of the genre's "cyberpunk" movement.

Gibson grew up in southwestern Virginia. After dropping out of high school in 1967, he traveled to Canada and eventually settled there, earning a B.A. (1977) from the University of British Columbia. Many of Gibson's early stories, including "Johnny Mnemonic" (1981; film 1995) and "Burning Chrome" (1982), were published in *Omni* magazine. With the publication of his first novel, *Neuromancer* (1984), Gibson emerged as a leading exponent of cyberpunk, a new school of science fiction writing. Cyberpunk combines a cynical, tough "punk" sensibility with futuristic cybernetic (i.e., having to do with communication and control theory) technology. Gibson's creation of "cyberspace," a computer-simulated reality that shows the nature of information, foreshadowed virtual reality technology and is considered the author's major contribution to the genre.

Neuromancer, which won three major science fiction awards (Nebula, Hugo, and Philip K. Dick), established Gibson's reputation. Its protagonist is a 22nd-century data thief who fights against the domination of a corporate-controlled society by breaking through the global computer network's cyberspace matrix. *Count Zero* (1986) was set in the same world as *Neuromancer* but seven years later. The characters of *Mona Lisa Overdrive* (1988) can "die" into computers, where they may support or sabotage outer reality. After collaborating with writer Bruce Sterling on *The Difference Engine* (1990), a story set in Victorian England, Gibson returned to the subject of cyberspace in *Virtual Light* (1993). His *Idoru* (1996), set in 21st-century Tokyo, focuses on the media and virtual celebrities of the future. *All Tomorrow's Parties* (1999) concerns a clairvoyant cyberpunk who labours to keep a villain from dominating the world. *Pattern Recognition* (2003) follows a marketing consultant who is hired to track down the origins of a mysterious Internet video. In *Spook Country* (2007), characters navigate a world filled with spies, ghosts, and other nefarious unseen agents.

JOHN HAWKES

(b. Aug. 17, 1925, Stamford, Conn., U.S.—d. May 15, 1998, Providence, R.I.)

The novels of John Hawkes achieve a dreamlike (often nightmarish) intensity through the suspension of traditional narrative constraints. He considered a story's structure his main concern, once stating in an interview that plot, character, and theme are "the true enemies of the novel."

Hawkes was an only child of a businessman. Between the ages of 10 and 15 years he lived in Alaska with his family, who then moved to New York City. Hawkes attended Harvard University, taking time out during World War II to serve as an ambulance driver in Italy and Germany but returning to achieve a B.A. in 1949. He worked at Harvard University Press from 1949 to 1955, then taught at Harvard until 1958 and for the next 30 years taught at Brown University.

Hawkes's first novel, *The Cannibal* (1949), depicts harbingers of a future apocalypse amid the rubble of postwar Germany. *The Beetle Leg* (1951) is a surreal parody of the pulp western. In 1954 he published two novellas, *The Goose on the Grave* and *The Owl*, both set in Italy.

With *The Lime Twig* (1961), a dark thriller set in postwar London, Hawkes attracted the critical attention that would place him in the front rank of avant-garde, postmodern American writers. His next novel, *Second Skin* (1964), is the first-person confessional of a retired naval officer. *The Blood Oranges* (1971; filmed 1997), *Death, Sleep, & the Traveler* (1974), and *Travesty* (1976) explore the concepts of marriage and freedom to unsettling effect. *The Passion Artist* (1979) and *Virginie: Her Two Lives* (1982) are tales of sexual obsession. Hawkes's later works include *Adventures in the Alaskan Skin Trade* (1985), whose narrator is a middle-aged woman; *Whistlejacket* (1988); *Sweet William: A Memoir of Old Horse* (1993), written in the voice of a horse; *The Frog* (1996); and *An Irish Eye* (1997), whose narrator is a 13-year-old female orphan. He also published *The Innocent Party* (1966), a collection of short plays, and *Lunar Landscapes*

(1969), a volume of short stories and novellas. *Humors of Blood & Skin: A John Hawkes Reader* was published in 1984.

Hawkes was little interested in plot, setting, or theme. His prose is poetic, irrational, and often comic. He said, "The imagination should always uncover new worlds for us. I want to try to create a world, not represent it."

OSCAR HIJUELOS

(b. August 24, 1951, New York, New York, U.S.)

Novelist Oscar Hijuelos's writing chronicles the pre-Castro Cuban immigrant experience in the United States, particularly in New York City.

Hijuelos attended City College of the City University of New York, where he received a B.A. in 1975 and an M.A. in 1976. He won critical acclaim for his first novel, *Our House in the Last World* (1983), and was awarded a Pulitzer Prize in 1990 for his second novel, *The Mambo Kings Play Songs of Love* (1989; filmed as *The Mambo Kings*, 1992). *Our House in the Last World* concerns members of the immigrant Santinio family who try to integrate into their Cuban identity and values the rhythms and culture of life in New York City's Spanish Harlem. In the novel Hijuelos employed surreal effects suggestive of modern Latin American fiction.

The Mambo Kings Play Songs of Love also chronicles Cuban immigrants, their quest for the American dream, and their eventual disillusionment. It vividly re-creates the musical and social environment of North America in the 1950s when the dance music of Cuban immigrants, the rumba and the mambo, began to achieve mainstream success. *Empress of the Splendid Season* (1999) continues the examination of immigrant life, this time revealing the discrepancy between the characters' rich self-images and their banal lives. Other novels by Hijuelos include *The Fourteen Sisters of Emilio Montez O'Brien* (1993), *Mr. Ives' Christmas* (1995), and *A Simple Habana Melody (From When the World Was Good)* (2002).

JACK KEROUAC

(b. March 12, 1922, Lowell, Mass..—d. Oct. 21, 1969, St. Petersburg, Fla.)

Jack Kerouac was an American novelist, poet, and leader of the Beat movement whose most famous book, *On the Road* (1957), had broad cultural influence before it was recognized for its literary merits. *On the Road* captured the spirit of its time like no 20th century work since F. Scott Fitzgerald's *The Great Gatsby* (1925).

CHILDHOOD AND EARLY INFLUENCES

Kerouac's mother worked in a shoe factory and his father worked as a printer in Lowell, Mass., a mill town with a large French Canadian population. Kerouac, who was born Jean-Louis Lebris de Kerouac, attended a French Canadian school in the morning and continued his studies in English in the afternoon. He spoke joual, a Canadian dialect of French, and so, though he was an American, he viewed his country as if he were a foreigner. Kerouac subsequently went to the Horace Mann School, a preparatory school in New York City, on a football scholarship. There he met Henri Cru, who helped Kerouac find jobs as a merchant seaman, and Seymour Wyse, who introduced Kerouac to jazz.

In 1940 Kerouac enrolled at Columbia University, where he met two writers who would become lifelong friends: Allen Ginsberg and William S. Burroughs. Together with Kerouac they are the seminal figures of the literary movement known as "Beat," a term introduced to Kerouac by Herbert Huncke, a Times Square junkie, petty thief, hustler, and writer.

Kerouac's childhood and early adulthood were marked by loss. His nine-year-old brother Gerard died in 1926. Kerouac's boyhood friend Sebastian Sampas died in 1944

Beat Movement

Also called the Beat generation, the Beat movement was an American social and literary movement originating in the 1950s and centred in the bohemian artist communities of San Francisco's North Beach, Los Angeles' Venice West, and New York City's Greenwich Village. Its adherents, self-styled as "beat" (originally meaning "weary," but later also connoting a musical sense, a "beatific" spirituality, and other meanings) and derisively called "beatniks," expressed their alienation from conventional, or "square," society by adopting an almost uniform style of seedy dress, manners, and "hip" vocabulary borrowed from jazz musicians. Generally apolitical and indifferent to social problems, they advocated personal release, purification, and illumination through the heightened sensory awareness that might be induced by drugs, jazz, sex, or the disciplines of Zen Buddhism. Apologists for the Beats, among them Paul Goodman, found the joylessness and purposelessness of modern society sufficient justification for both withdrawal and protest.

Beat poets sought to liberate poetry from academic preciosity and bring it "back to the streets." They read their poetry, sometimes to the accompaniment of progressive jazz, in such Beat strongholds as the Coexistence Bagel Shop and Lawrence Ferlinghetti's City Lights bookstore in San Francisco. The verse was frequently chaotic and liberally sprinkled with obscenities but was sometimes, as in the case of Allen Ginsberg's *Howl* (1956), ruggedly powerful and moving. Ginsberg and other major figures of the movement, such as the novelist Jack Kerouac, advocated a kind of free, unstructured composition in which the writer put down his thoughts and feelings without plan or revision — to convey the immediacy of experience — an approach that led to the production of much undisciplined and incoherent verbiage on the part of their imitators. By about 1960, when the faddish notoriety of the movement had begun to fade, it had produced a number of interesting and promising writers, including Ferlinghetti, Gregory Corso, Philip Whalen, and Gary Snyder, and had paved the way for acceptance of other unorthodox and previously ignored writers, such as the Black Mountain poets and the novelist William Burroughs.

and his father, Leo, in 1946. In a deathbed promise to Leo, Kerouac pledged to care for his mother, Gabrielle, affectionately known as Memere. Kerouac married three times: Edie Parker (1944; annulled 1946); Joan Haverty (1951), with whom he had a daughter, Jan Michelle; and Stella Sampas (1966), the sister of Sebastian, who had died at Anzio, Italy, during World War II.

ON THE ROAD AND OTHER EARLY WORK

By the time Kerouac and Burroughs met in 1944, Kerouac had already written a million words. His boyhood ambition had been to write the "great American novel." His first novel, *The Town & the City* (1950), received favourable reviews but was considered derivative of the novels of Thomas Wolfe, whose *Time and the River* (1935) and *You Can't Go Home Again* (1940) were then popular. In his novel Kerouac articulated the "New Vision," that "everything was collapsing," a theme that would dominate his grand design to have all his work taken together as "one vast book," which he dubbed *The Legend of Duluoz*.

Yet Kerouac was unhappy with the pace of his prose. The music of bebop jazz artists Thelonious Monk and Charlie Parker began to drive Kerouac toward his "spontaneous bop prosody," as Ginsberg later called it, which took shape in the late 1940s through various drafts of his second novel, *On the Road*. The original manuscript, a scroll written in a three-week blast in 1951, is legendary: Composed of approximately 120 feet (37 metres) of paper taped together and fed into a manual typewriter, the

Eager to keep up a hasty writing pace echoing 1940s bebop music, Jack Kerouac typed his On the Road manuscript over a three-week period on a 120-foot scroll. Don Emmert/AFP/Getty Images

scroll allowed Kerouac the fast pace he was hoping to achieve. He also hoped to publish the novel as a scroll so that the reader would not be encumbered by having to turn the pages of a book. Rejected for publication at first, it finally was printed in 1957. In the interim, Kerouac wrote several more "true-life" novels, *Doctor Sax* (1959), *Maggie Cassidy* (1959), and *Tristessa* (1960) among them.

Kerouac found himself a national sensation after *On the Road* received a rave review from the *New York Times* critic Gilbert Millstein. Millstein extolled the literary merits of the book, but to the American public the novel represented a departure from tradition. Kerouac, though, was disappointed with having achieved fame for what he considered the wrong reason: Little attention went to the excellence of his writing and more to the novel's radically different characters and its characterization of hipsters and their nonconformist celebration of sex, jazz, and endless movement. The character Dean Moriarty (based on Neal Cassady, another important influence on Kerouac's style) was an American archetype, embodying "IT," an intense moment of heightened experience achieved through fast driving, talking, or "blowing" (as a horn player might) or in writing. In *On the Road* Sal Paradise explains his fascination with others who have "IT," such as Dean Moriarty and Rollo Greb as well as jazz performers: "The only ones for me are the mad ones, the ones who are mad to live, mad to talk, mad to be saved." These are characters for whom the perpetual now is all.

Readers often confused Kerouac with Sal Paradise, the amoral hipster at the centre of his novel. The critic Norman Podhoretz famously wrote that Beat writing was an assault against the intellect and against decency. This misreading dominated negative reactions to *On the Road*. Kerouac's rebellion, however, is better understood as a quest for the solidity of home and family, what he considered "the hearthside ideal." He wanted to achieve in his writing that which he could find neither in the promise of America nor in the empty spirituality of Roman Catholicism; he strived instead for the serenity that he had discovered in his adopted Buddhism. Kerouac felt that the Beat label marginalized him and prevented him from being treated as he wanted to be treated, as a man of letters in the American tradition of Herman Melville and Walt Whitman.

LATER WORK

By the 1960s Kerouac had finished most of the writing for which he is best known. In 1961 he wrote *Big Sur* in 10 days while living in the cabin of Lawrence Ferlinghetti, a fellow Beat poet, in California's Big Sur region. Two years later Kerouac's account of his brother's death was published as the spiritual *Visions of Gerard*. Another important autobiographical book, *Vanity of Duluoz* (1968), recounts stories of his childhood, his schooling, and the dramatic scandals that defined early Beat legend.

In 1969 Kerouac was broke, and many of his books were out of print. An alcoholic, he was living with his third wife and his mother in St. Petersburg, Fla., where he spent his time in local bars. A week after he had been beaten by fellow drinkers whom he had antagonized, he died of internal hemorrhaging in front of his television while watching *The Galloping Gourmet* — the ultimate ending for a writer who came to be known as the "martyred king of the Beats."

STEPHEN KING

(b. Sept. 21, 1947, Portland, Maine)

Author Stephen King has been credited with reviving the genre of horror fiction in the late 20th century.

King graduated from the University of Maine in 1970 with a bachelor's degree in English. While writing short stories, he supported himself by teaching and working as a janitor, among other jobs. His first published novel, *Carrie* (film 1976), about a tormented teenage girl gifted with telekinetic powers, appeared in 1974 and was an immediate popular success. *Carrie* was the first of many novels in which King blended horror, the macabre, fantasy, and science fiction. Among such works were *Salem's Lot* (1975), *The*

Shining (1977; film 1980), *The Stand* (1978), *The Dead Zone* (1979; film 1983), *Firestarter* (1980; film 1984), *Cujo* (1981; film 1983), *The Running Man* (1982; film 1987), *Christine* (1983; film 1983), *Thinner* (1984; film 1996), *It* (1986), *Misery* (1987; film 1990), *The Tommyknockers* (1987), *The Dark Half* (1989; film 1993), *Needful Things* (1991; film 1993), *Gerald's Game* (1992), *Dolores Claiborne* (1993; film 1995), *Insomnia* (1994), *The Girl Who Loved Tom Gordon* (2000), *Dreamcatcher* (2001; film 2003), and *Cell* (2006). Several of these works, including *The Dead Zone* and *The Running Man*, appeared under the pseudonym Richard Bachmann.

King is also the author of a serial novel, *The Dark Tower*, whose first installment, *The Gunslinger*, appeared in 1982. A seventh volume was published in 2004.

In his books King has explored almost every terror-producing theme imaginable, from vampires, rabid dogs, deranged killers, and a pyromaniac to ghosts, extrasensory perception and telekinesis, biological warfare, and even a malevolent automobile. In his later fiction, exemplified by *Gerald's Game* and *Dolores Claiborne*, King departed from the horror genre to work instead at providing sharply detailed psychological portraits of his major characters, many of them women, who confront difficult and challenging circumstances.

Though his work sometimes has been disparaged as undisciplined and inelegant, King is a talented storyteller whose books gain their effect from realistic detail, forceful plotting, and the author's undoubted ability to involve and scare the reader. His work consistently addresses such themes as the potential for politics and technology to disrupt or even destroy an individual human life. Obsession, the forms it can assume, and its power to wreck individuals, families, and whole communities is a recurring theme in King's fiction, driving the narratives of *Christine*, *Misery*, and *Needful Things*.

By the early 1990s, King's books had sold more than 100 million copies worldwide, and his name had become synonymous with the genre of horror fiction. He also wrote short stories collected in such volumes as *Night Shift* (1978) and *Just After Sunset* (2008) and penned several novellas and motion-picture screenplays. Some of his novels have been adapted for the screen by such directors as John Carpenter, David Cronenberg, Brian De Palma, Stanley Kubrick, and Rob Reiner.

King explored both his own career and the craft of writing in *On Writing* (2000), a book he completed as he was recovering from severe injuries received after being struck by a car. King experimented with different forms of book distribution: *The Plant* was released in 2000 solely as an e-book, distributed via the Internet, with readers asked but not required to pay for it, and the novella *Ur* was made available in 2009 only to users of the Kindle electronic reading device.

MAXINE HONG KINGSTON
(b. Oct. 27, 1940, Stockton, Calif.)

Much of Maxine Hong Kingston's work is rooted in her experience as a first-generation Chinese American.

Maxine Hong was the eldest of six American-born children of Chinese immigrant parents. Hong's father, a scholar, had left China in 1924 and immigrated to New York City. Unable to find work as a poet or calligrapher, he took a job in a laundry. Hong's mother had remained behind in China and joined him in the United States in 1939.

Hong attended the University of California, Berkeley, as a scholarship student, graduating in 1962. At Berkeley she met aspiring actor Earll Kingston. They were married in November 1962 and had a son in 1964. The couple taught at Sunset High School in 1966–67 in Hayward, Calif., then moved to Hawaii, where she held a series of teaching jobs for the next 10 years.

In 1976 Kingston published her first book, *Woman Warrior: Memoirs of a Girlhood Among Ghosts*. It combines myth, family history, folktales, and memories of the experience of growing up within two conflicting cultures. The book was an immediate critical success, winning the 1976 National Book Critics' Circle Award for nonfiction. In her second memoir, *China Men* (1980), Kingston tells the story of Chinese immigration through the experiences of the men in her family. Using the narrative techniques of *Woman Warrior*, she relates their stories of virtual slave labour, loneliness, and discrimination. *China Men* won the American Book Award for nonfiction. In *Tripmaster Monkey: His Fake Book* (1989), the main character— Whittman Ah Sing, named after Walt Whitman—narrates a peculiarly 20th-century American odyssey. The book combines Eastern and Western literary traditions while emphasizing the Americanness of its characters. In *To Be the Poet* (2002), written mainly in verse, Kingston presented a rumination on elements of her own past and the acts of reading and creating poetry. *The Fifth Book of Peace* (2003) combines elements of fiction and memoir in the manner of a Chinese talk-story, a tradition in which elements of both the real and imagined worlds become interpolated.

Kingston also published poems, short stories, and articles. Her collection of 12 prose sketches, *Hawai'i One Summer* (1987), was published in a limited edition with original woodblock prints and calligraphy. Beginning in 1993 Kingston ran a series of writing and meditation workshops for veterans of various conflicts and their families. From these workshops came the material for *Veterans of War, Veterans of Peace* (2006), a collection edited by Kingston containing prose and verse on the experiences of war, domestic violence, drug abuse, and other traumatic experiences.

BERNARD MALAMUD

(b. April 26, 1914, Brooklyn, N.Y.—d. March 18, 1986, New York, N.Y.)

Bernard Malamud made parables out of Jewish immigrant life. Malamud's parents were Russian Jews who had fled tsarist Russia. He was born to a poor family in Brooklyn, where his father owned a small grocery store. Malamud's mother died when he was 15 years old. Early on he assumed responsibility for his handicapped brother and was unhappy when his father remarried. Malamud was educated at the City College of New York (B.A., 1936) and Columbia University (M.A., 1942). He taught at high schools in New York City (1940–49), at Oregon State University (1949–61), and at Bennington College in Vermont (1961–66, 1968–86).

His first novel, *The Natural* (1952; film 1984), is a fable about a baseball hero who is gifted with miraculous powers. *The Assistant* (1957) is about a young Gentile hoodlum and an old Jewish grocer, and *The Fixer* (1966) takes place in tsarist Russia. The story of a Jewish handyman unjustly imprisoned for the murder of a Christian boy, it won Malamud a Pulitzer Prize. His other novels are *A New Life* (1961), *The Tenants* (1971), *Dubin's Lives* (1979), and *God's Grace* (1982).

Malamud's genius is most apparent in his short stories. Although told in a spare, compressed prose that reflects the terse speech of their immigrant characters, the stories often burst into emotional, metaphorical language. Grim city neighbourhoods are visited by magical events, and their hardworking residents are given glimpses of love and self-sacrifice. Malamud's short-story collections are *The Magic Barrel* (1958), *Idiots First* (1963), *Pictures of Fidelman* (1969), and *Rembrandt's Hat* (1973). *The Stories of Bernard Malamud* appeared in 1983, and *The People and Uncollected Stories* was published posthumously in 1989. *The People*, an unfinished novel, tells the story of a Jewish immigrant adopted by a 19th-century American Indian tribe. One critic spoke of "its moral sinew and its delicacy of tone."

CORMAC MCCARTHY

(b. July 20, 1933, Providence, R.I.)

Cormac McCarthy is known for his works in the Southern gothic tradition. His novels about wayward characters in the rural American South and Southwest are noted for their dark violence, dense prose, and stylistic complexity.

Charles McCarthy, Jr., attended the University of Tennessee at Knoxville and served in the U.S. Air Force from 1953 to 1956. Readers were first introduced to McCarthy's difficult narrative style in the novel *The Orchard Keeper* (1965), about a Tennessee man and his two mentors. Social outcasts highlight such novels as *Outer Dark* (1968), about two incestuous siblings; *Child of God* (1974), about a lonely man's descent into depravity; and *Suttree* (1979), about a man who overcomes his fixation on death.

McCarthy's *Blood Meridian* (1985), a violent frontier tale, was a critical sensation, hailed as his masterpiece. *Blood Meridian* tells the story of a 14-year-old boy who joins a gang of outlaws hunting Native Americans along the U.S.-Mexico border in the 1840s. The group is headed by a malevolent figure called the Judge, who leads the gang through a series of staggeringly amoral actions, through which McCarthy explores the nature of good and evil.

McCarthy achieved popular fame with *All the Pretty Horses* (1992; film 2000), winner of the National Book

Award. The first volume of *The Border Trilogy*, it is the coming-of-age story of John Grady Cole, a Texan who travels to Mexico. The second installment, *The Crossing* (1994), set before and during World War II, follows the picaresque adventures of brothers Billy and Boyd Parham and centres around three round-trip passages that Billy makes between southwestern New Mexico and Mexico. The trilogy concludes with *Cities of the Plain* (1998), which interweaves the lives of John Grady Cole and Billy Parham through their employment on a ranch in New Mexico.

McCarthy's later works include *No Country for Old Men* (2005; film 2007), a modern, bloody western that opens with a drug deal gone bad. In the postapocalyptic *The Road* (2006; Pulitzer Prize; film 2009), a father and son struggle to survive after a disaster, left unspecified, that has all but destroyed the United States. McCarthy also wrote the plays *The Stonemason* (2001) and *The Sunset Limited* (2006).

MARY MCCARTHY

(b. June 21, 1912, Seattle, Wash.—d. Oct. 25, 1989, New York, N.Y.)

Mary McCarthy was an American critic and novelist whose fiction is noted for its wit and acerbity in analyzing the finer moral nuances of intellectual dilemmas.

McCarthy, whose family belonged to all three major American religious traditions—Protestant, Roman Catholic, and Jewish—was left an orphan at age six. After her parents' deaths, she spent several unhappy years with strict relatives in Minnesota before going to live with her grandparents in Seattle, Wash., under conditions she found more pleasant. Her unhappiness with her orthodox Roman Catholic relatives in Minnesota did not erase her interest in Catholicism, which lasted long after she lost her faith. McCarthy was educated at private schools and at Vassar College (B.A., 1933). She then worked as a critic for the *New Republic*, the *Nation*, and the *Partisan Review,* where she served on the editorial staff from 1937 to 1948. For that publication she wrote extensively on art, theatre, travel, and politics. She married four times, the second time, in 1938, to the noted American critic Edmund Wilson, who encouraged her to begin writing fiction.

As both a novelist and a critic McCarthy was noted for bitingly satiric commentaries on marriage, sexual expression, the impotence of intellectuals, and the role of women in contemporary urban America. Her first story, "Cruel and Barbarous Treatment," was published in the *Southern Review* in 1939. It later became the opening chapter of *The Company She Keeps* (1942), a loosely connected series of semiautobiographical stories concerning a fashionable woman who experiences divorce and psychoanalysis. *The Oasis* (1949; also published as *Source of Embarrassment*) is a short novel about the failure of a utopian community of ineffectually idealistic intellectuals. In *The Groves of Academe* (1952), McCarthy satirized American higher education during the Joseph McCarthy era. In 1956 and 1959 McCarthy experimented with lavishly photographed travelogues of Italy in *Venice, Observed* and *The Stones of Florence*. Her autobiographical *Memories of a Catholic Girlhood* (1957) was highly praised by critics. It was followed by *The Group* (1963), the novel for which McCarthy is perhaps best known. The book follows eight Vassar women of the class of 1933 through their subsequent careers and the intellectual fads of the 1930s and '40s and became the most popular of all her works and was made into a film in 1966. McCarthy's controversial series of essays on the Vietnam War first appeared in the *New York Review of Books* and was later collected in *Vietnam* (1967) and *Hanoi* (1968). Her other books include the novel *Birds of America* (1971); *The Mask of State* (1974), on the Watergate affair; *Cannibals and Missionaries* (1979), a novel;

and *How I Grew* (1987), a second volume of autobiography. An unfinished autobiography, *Intellectual Memoirs, New York, 1936–38*, was published posthumously in 1992. *Between Friends: The Correspondence of Hannah Arendt and Mary McCarthy, 1949–1975* (1995) is a record of McCarthy's long friendship with the German-born American political scientist and philosopher Hannah Arendt.

ANAÏS NIN

(b. Feb. 21, 1903, Neuilly, France — d. Jan. 14, 1977, Los Angeles, Calif.)

Anaïs Nin was a French-born author of novels and short stories whose literary reputation rests on the eight

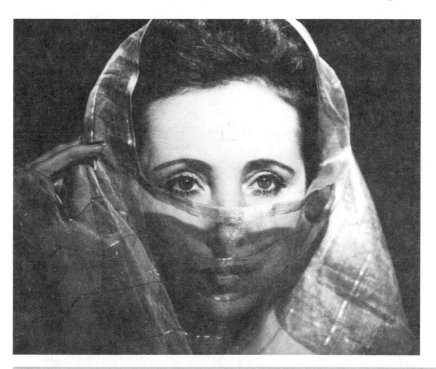

The publication of her diaries finally garnered Anaïs Nin more widespread praise and recognition for her novels, including the five-volume continuous novel Cities of the Interior. Library of Congress, Prints & Photographs Division, NYWT&S Collection

published volumes of her personal diaries. Her writing shows the influence of the Surrealist movement and her study of psychoanalysis under Otto Rank.

Brought to New York City by her mother in 1914, Nin was educated there but later returned to Europe. She launched her literary career with the publication of *D.H. Lawrence: An Unprofessional Study* (1932); the book led to a lifelong friendship with the American author Henry Miller.

At the beginning of World War II Nin returned to New York City. There she continued—at her own expense—to print and publish her novels and short stories, and, although no critical acclaim was forthcoming, her works were admired by many leading literary figures of the time. Not until 1966, with the appearance of the first volume of her diaries, did she win recognition as a writer of significance. The success of the diary provoked interest in her earlier work *Cities of the Interior* (1959), a five-volume *roman-fleuve*, or continuous novel, which consists of *Ladders to Fire* (1946), *Children of the Albatross* (1947), *The Four-Chambered Heart* (1950), *A Spy in the House of Love* (1954), and *Solar Barque* (1958).

Nin's literary contribution was a subject of controversy in her lifetime and remained so after her death. Many critics admired her unique expression of femininity, her lyrical style, and her psychological insight. Some dismissed her concern with her own fulfillment as self-indulgent and narcissistic. Opinion was further divided by the posthumous *Delta of Venus: Erotica* (1977) and later collections of previously unpublished erotic stories written on commission during the financially lean years of the early 1940s. Her other works of fiction include a collection of short stories, *Under a Glass Bell* (1944); the novels *House of Incest* (1936), *Seduction of the Minotaur* (1961),

and *Collages* (1964); and three novelettes collected in
Winter of Artifice (1939).

TIM O'BRIEN

(b. Oct. 1, 1946, Austin, Minn.)

William Timothy O'Brien is noted for his writings about
American soldiers in the Vietnam War.

After studying political science at Macalester College,
St. Paul, Minn. (B.A., 1968), O'Brien fought in Vietnam.
When he returned to the United States, he studied inter-
mittently at Harvard University and worked for the
Washington Post (1971–74) as an intern and reporter. He collected his newspaper and magazine articles about his war
experiences in his first book, *If I Die in a Combat Zone, Box
Me Up and Ship Me Home* (1973). By turns meditative and
brutally realistic, it was praised for its honest portrayal of
a soldier's emotions.

The Vietnam War is present in many of O'Brien's
novels. One of the two protagonists in *Northern Lights*
(1975) is a wounded war hero. Set in an isolated,
snow-covered part of Minnesota during a disastrous
cross-country ski trip, the novel is an examination of
courage. In *Going After Cacciato* (1978), a soldier abandons his platoon in Vietnam to try to walk to Paris, and a
fellow soldier escapes the war's horrors by inventing
elaborate fantasies about his journey. A man's lifelong
fear of dying from a nuclear bombing is the subject of
The Nuclear Age (1981), while *The Things They Carried*
(1990) and *In the Lake of the Woods* (1994) return to the subject of the experiences and effects of the Vietnam War.
O'Brien's writing took a new turn with publication of
Tomcat in Love (1999), a nuanced comic novel about the
search for love.

CYNTHIA OZICK

(b. April 17, 1928, New York, N.Y.)

The American novelist, short-story writer, essayist, and intellectual Cynthia Ozick produced works that seek to define the challenge of remaining Jewish in contemporary American life. By delving into the oldest religious sources of Judaism, Ozick explored much new territory.

Ozick received a B.A. in English in 1949 from New York University and an M.A. in 1950 from Ohio State University. Her first novel, *Trust* (1966), is the story of a woman's rejection of her wealthy American Jewish family and her search for her renegade father in Europe. It has echoes of Henry James in its juxtaposition of American and European settings. In subsequent books, such as *Bloodshed and Three Novellas* (1976), Ozick struggled with the idea that the creation of art (a pagan activity) is in direct opposition to principles of Judaism, which forbids the creation of idols.

The psychological aftermath of the Holocaust is another theme of her work, especially in *Levitation: Five Fictions* (1982) and the novels *The Cannibal Galaxy* (1983) and *The Shawl* (1989). She often drew on traditional Jewish mysticism to expand upon her themes. With her recurring character Ruth Puttermesser, in 1997 she published *The Puttermesser Papers*, a short novel consisting of narratives and false memories of the aging Puttermesser, who in one story brings a female golem to life to save New York City, with disastrous results.

Ozick's later works turn away from the theme of the sacred and the profane. Her novel *The Messiah of Stockholm* (1987) is, in part, a meditation on the nature of writing. *Heir to the Glimmering World* (2004; also published as *The Bear Boy*) tells the story of a young woman hired as a nanny in the home of two Jewish-German academics exiled to

New York City in the 1930s. *Diction: A Quartet*, a collection of four short stories, was published in 2008.

Many of Ozick's essays have been collected in *Art & Ardor* (1983), *Metaphor & Memory* (1989), *Fame & Folly* (1996), *Quarrel & Quandary* (2000), and *The Din in the Head* (2006).

J.D. SALINGER

(b. Jan. 1, 1919, New York, N.Y.—d. Jan. 27, 2010, Cornish, N.H.)

J.D. Salinger is best known for his novel *The Catcher in the Rye* (1951), which won critical acclaim and devoted admirers, especially among the post–World War II generation of college students. His entire corpus of published works consists of that one novel and 13 short stories, all originally written in the period 1948–59.

Jerome David Salinger was the son of a Jewish father and a Christian mother, and, like Holden Caulfield, the hero of *The Catcher in the Rye,* he grew up in New York City, attending public schools and a military academy. After brief periods at New York and Columbia universities, he devoted himself entirely to writing, and his stories began to appear in periodicals in 1940. After his return from service in the U.S. Army (1942–46), Salinger's name and writing style became increasingly associated with the *New Yorker* magazine, which published almost all of his later stories. Some of the best of these made use of his wartime experiences. "For Esmé—With Love and Squalor" (1950) describes a U.S. soldier's poignant encounter with two British children. "A Perfect Day for Bananafish" (1948) concerns the suicide of the sensitive, despairing veteran Seymour Glass.

Major critical and popular recognition came with the publication of *The Catcher in the Rye,* whose central character, a sensitive, rebellious adolescent, relates in authentic teenage idiom his flight from the "phony" adult world, his search for innocence and truth, and his final collapse on a psychiatrist's couch. The humour and colourful language of *The Catcher in the Rye* place it in the tradition of Mark Twain's *Adventures of Huckleberry Finn* and the stories of Ring Lardner, but its hero, like most of Salinger's child characters, views his life with an added dimension of precocious self-consciousness. *Nine Stories* (1953), a selection of Salinger's best work, added to his reputation.

The reclusive habits of Salinger in his later years made his personal life a matter of speculation among devotees, while his small literary output was a subject of controversy among critics. *Franny and Zooey* (1961) brought together two earlier *New Yorker* stories. Both deal with the Glass family, as do the two stories in *Raise High the Roof Beam, Carpenters; and Seymour: An Introduction* (1963).

MICKEY SPILLANE

(b. March 9, 1918, Brooklyn, N.Y.—d. July 17, 2006, Murrells Inlet, S.C.)

Mickey Spillane is the pseudonym of Frank Morrison Spillane, a writer of detective fiction, whose popular work is characterized by violence and sexual licentiousness.

Spillane began his career by writing for pulp magazines and comic books to pay for his schooling. His first novel, *I, The Jury* (1947), introduced detective Mike Hammer, who appeared in other works, such as *My Gun Is Quick* (1950) and *The Big Kill* (1951). *Kiss Me, Deadly* (1952) was made into a highly successful movie (1955). In the early 1950s Spillane retired from writing after he became a Jehovah's Witness. Ten years later he resumed his career with *The Deep* (1961).

Spillane returned to the Mike Hammer series with *The Girl Hunters* (1962). He also wrote the script for and played the role of Hammer in the novel's film adaptation (1963). Later books in the series include *The Killing Man* (1989) and *Black Alley* (1996). In addition to movies, the Mike Hammer character was also featured in two popular television series. Spillane initiated a new book series with *Day of the Guns* (1964), which centred on the international agent Tiger Mann. Among his other books are *The Last Cop Out* (1973) and the children's book *The Day the Sea Rolled Back* (1979).

Spillane, who claimed to write solely for monetary gain, flouted literary taste with recurring elements of sadism that disturbed some readers, but the captivating vigour of his narrative and his central characters brought him popular success.

WALLACE STEGNER

(b. Feb. 18, 1909, Lake Mills, Iowa—d. April 13, 1993, Santa Fe, N.M.)

Wallace Stegner was an author of fiction and historical nonfiction set mainly in the western United States. All his writings are informed by a deep sense of the American experience and the potential, which he termed "the geography of promise," that the West symbolizes.

Stegner grew up in Saskatchewan, Can., and in several western states. He received a B.A. degree (1930) from the University of Utah and an M.A. (1932) and a Ph.D. (1935) from the University of Iowa. He taught at several universities, notably Stanford University, where from 1945 to 1971 he directed the creative writing program. His first novel, *Remembering Laughter* (1937), like his next three novels, was a relatively short work. His fifth novel, *The Big Rock Candy Mountain* (1943), the story of an American family moving from place to place in the West, seeking their fortune, was his first critical and popular success. Among his later novels are *The Preacher and the Slave* (1950; later titled *Joe Hill:*

A Biographical Novel), the best-selling *A Shooting Star* (1961), *Recapitulation* (1979), and *Crossing to Safety* (1987).

His *Angle of Repose* (1971) won a Pulitzer Prize. The novel tells two stories. The framing narrative concerns a disabled historian named Lyman Ward who has been abandoned by his wife and is forced to interact with members of the 1960s counterculture that he loathes, but the primary narrative is Ward's account of his grandparents' 19th-century sojourn through a number of Western mining camps. *The Spectator Bird* (1976), which won a National Book Award, has a similar two-narrative structure that alternates between a contemporary account of an aged literary agent upset with American culture and his flashback of a visit to Denmark he and his wife made 20 years earlier.

Stegner's nonfiction includes two histories of the Mormon settlement of Utah, *Mormon Country* (1942) and *The Gathering of Zion: The Story of the Mormon Trail* (1964); a biography of Western explorer-naturalist John Wesley Powell, *Beyond the Hundredth Meridian* (1954); and a history of the early years of oil drilling in the Middle East, *Discovery!: The Search for Arabian Oil* (1971). A book of essays, *Where the Bluebird Sings to the Lemonade Springs: Living and Writing in the West*, was published in 1992.

WILLIAM STYRON

(b. June 11, 1925, Newport News, Va.—d. Nov. 1, 2006, Martha's Vineyard, Mass.)

The novelist William Styron was noted for his treatment of tragic themes and use of a rich, classical prose style.

Styron served in the U.S. Marine Corps before graduating from Duke University, Durham, N.C., in 1947. During the 1950s he was part of the community of American expatriates in Paris, and in 1953 he became an advisory editor to the *Paris Review*.

Styron's first novel, *Lie Down in Darkness* (1951), set in his native tidewater Virginia, tells of a young woman from a loveless middle-class family who fights unsuccessfully for her sanity before committing suicide. His next work, *The Long March* (1956), chronicles a brutal forced march undertaken by recruits in a Marine training camp. The novel *Set This House on Fire*, complexly structured and set largely in Italy, appeared in 1960.

Styron's fourth novel, *The Confessions of Nat Turner* (1967), is an account of a historical incident, a slave rebellion led by the title character in Virginia in 1831. Based on a transcript of Turner's testimony and told from his point of view, the book sympathetically portrays a man who is denied happiness because of his degrading enslavement. Embittered and alienated, he undertakes a bloody revolt that ends in his capture and execution. The novel's publication at the peak of the civil rights movement helped make it a best seller. It was awarded a Pulitzer Prize in 1968, but it also stirred wide controversy, with critics accusing the book of racism and of misrepresenting African American history.

Styron's final novel, *Sophie's Choice* (1979; film 1982), portrays the growth of a friendship between a young Southern writer and a Roman Catholic woman from Poland who survived the Nazi death camp Auschwitz. It, too, became a controversial best seller. His other works include the play *In the Clap Shack* (1972) and *This Quiet Dust* (1982), a collection of essays that treat the dominant themes of Styron's fiction. *Darkness Visible* (1990) is a non-fiction account of Styron's struggle against depression. *A Tidewater Morning* (1993) consists of autobiographical stories. *Havanas in Camelot* (2008), a collection of personal essays on topics ranging from the author's friendship with Pres. John F. Kennedy to his morning walks with his dog, was published posthumously.

Known for his multilayered plots, David Foster Wallace wrote intricate novels that were both witty and poetic. Steve Liss/Time & Life Pictures/Getty Images

DAVID FOSTER WALLACE

(b. Feb. 21, 1962, Ithaca, N.Y.—Sept. 12, 2008, Claremont, Calif.)

The novelist, short-story writer, and essayist David Foster Wallace wrote dense works that provide a dark, often satirical analysis of American culture.

Wallace was the son of a philosophy professor and an English teacher. He received a B.A. from Amherst College in 1985. He was completing a master's degree in creative writing at the University of Arizona when his highly regarded debut novel, *The Broom of the System* (1987), was published. He later taught creative writing at Illinois State University and at Pomona College. He received a MacArthur Foundation Fellowship grant in 1997.

Wallace became best known for his second novel, *Infinite Jest* (1996), a massive, multilayered novel that he wrote over the course of four years. In it appear a sweeping cast of postmodern characters that range from recovering alcoholics and foreign statesmen to residents of a halfway house and high-school tennis stars. Presenting a futuristic vision of a world in which advertising has become omnipresent, *Infinite Jest* takes place during calendar years that have been named by companies that purchased the rights to promote their products. Critics, who found Wallace's dense writing style variously exhilarating and maddening, compared *Infinite Jest* with the novels of Thomas Pynchon and Don DeLillo.

Wallace's short stories are collected in *Girl with Curious Hair* (1989), *Brief Interviews with Hideous Men* (1999), and *Oblivion* (2004). His essay collections include *A Supposedly Fun Thing I'll Never Do Again* (1997) and *Consider the Lobster, and Other Essays* (2005). *Everything and More: A Compact History of Infinity* (2003) is a survey of the mathematical concept of infinity. He also wrote, with Mark Costello, *Signifying Rappers: Rap and Race in the Urban Present* (1990; 2nd ed. 1997). Wallace's death was an apparent suicide.

TOM WOLFE

(b. March 2, 1930, Richmond, Va.)

The novelist, journalist, and social commentator Tom Wolfe is best known as a leading critic of contemporary life and a proponent of new journalism (the application of fiction-writing techniques to journalism).

After studying at Washington and Lee University (B.A., 1951) and Yale University (Ph.D., 1957), Wolfe wrote for several newspapers, including the *Springfield Union* in Massachusetts and the *Washington Post*. He later worked as an editor on such magazines as *New York* and *Esquire* (from 1977) and as an artist for *Harper's*.

His first book, *The Kandy-Kolored Tangerine-Flake Streamline Baby* (1964), is a collection of essays satirizing American trends and celebrities of the 1960s. *The Electric Kool-Aid Acid Test* (1968) chronicles the psychedelic drug culture of the 1960s. His other works include *Radical Chic & Mau-Mauing the Flak Catchers* (1970), *The Painted Word* (1975), *From Bauhaus to Our House* (1981), *The Worship of Art: Notes on the New God* (1984), and *A Man in Full* (1998). *The Right Stuff* (1979; film 1983), which examines aspects of the first U.S. astronaut program, and *The Bonfire of the Vanities* (1987; film 1990), a novel of urban greed and corruption, were bestsellers.

Wolfe's *Hooking Up* (2000) is a collection of fiction and essays, all previously published except for "My Three Stooges," a scandalous diatribe about John Updike, Norman Mailer, and John Irving, who had all been critical of *A Man in Full*. Wolfe's third novel, *I Am Charlotte Simmons* (2004), examines modern-day student life at fictional Dupont University through the eyes of small-town protagonist Charlotte Simmons.

CHAPTER 3

POETRY AFTER WORLD WAR II

The post–World War II years produced an abundance of strong poetry but no individual poet as dominant and accomplished as T.S. Eliot, Ezra Pound, Wallace Stevens, Robert Frost, or William Carlos Williams, whose long careers were coming to an end. The major poetry from 1945 to 1960 was Modernist in its ironic texture yet formal in its insistence on regular rhyme and metre. Beginning in the late 1950s, however, there were a variety of poets and schools who rebelled against these constraints and experimented with more-open forms and more-colloquial styles.

FORMAL POETS

The leading figure of the late 1940s was Robert Lowell. Influenced by Eliot and such Metaphysical poets as John Donne and Gerard Manley Hopkins, Lowell explored his spiritual torments and family history in *Lord Weary's Castle* (1946).

Lowell was born in 1917 and grew up in Boston. James Russell Lowell was his great-granduncle, and Amy, Percival, and A. Lawrence Lowell were distant cousins. Although he turned away from his Puritan heritage — largely because he was repelled by what he felt was the high value it placed on the accumulation of money — his continual fascination with it forms the subject of many of

Robert Lowell was one of the foremost formal poets of the 1940s. His work runs the gamut from tumultuous, particularly in his early work, to tranquil. Alfred Eisenstaedt/Time & Life Pictures/Getty Images

his poems. Lowell attended Harvard University, but, after falling under the influence of the Southern formalist school of poetry, he transferred to Kenyon College in Gambier, Ohio, where he studied with John Crowe Ransom, a leading exponent of the Fugitives, and began a lifelong friendship with Randall Jarrell. Lowell graduated in 1940 and that year married the novelist Jean Stafford and converted temporarily to Roman Catholicism. After being divorced in 1948, Lowell married the writer and critic Elizabeth Hardwick the next year (divorced 1972). His third wife was the Irish journalist and novelist Lady Caroline Blackwood, whom he married in 1972.

During World War II, Lowell was sentenced, for conscientious objection, to a year and a day in the federal penitentiary at Danbury, Conn., and he served five months of his sentence. His poem "In the Cage" from *Lord Weary's*

Castle (1946) comments on this experience, as does in greater detail "Memories of West Street and Lepke" in *Life Studies* (1959). His first volume of poems, *Land of Unlikeness* (1944), deals with a world in crisis and the hunger for spiritual security. *Lord Weary's Castle*, which won the Pulitzer Prize in 1947, exhibits greater variety and command. It contains two of his most praised poems: "The Quaker Graveyard in Nantucket," elegizing Lowell's cousin Warren Winslow, lost at sea during World War II, and "Colloquy in Black Rock," celebrating the feast of Corpus Christi. In 1947 Lowell was named poetry consultant to the Library of Congress (now poet laureate consultant in poetry), a position he held for one year.

In 1951 he published a book of dramatic monologues, *Mills of the Kavanaughs*. After a few years abroad, Lowell settled in Boston in 1954. His *Life Studies* (1959), which won the National Book Award for poetry, contains an autobiographical essay, "91 Revere Street," as well as a series of 15 confessional poems. Chief among these are "Waking in the Blue," which tells of his confinement in a mental hospital, and "Skunk Hour," which conveys his mental turmoil with dramatic intensity.

Lowell's activities in the civil rights and antiwar campaigns of the 1960s lent a more public note to his next three books of poetry: *For the Union Dead* (1964), *Near the Ocean* (1967), and *Notebook 1967–68* (1969). The last-named work is a poetic record of a tumultuous year in the poet's life and exhibits the interrelation between politics, the individual, and his culture. Lowell's trilogy of plays, *The Old Glory*, which views American culture over the span of history, was published in 1965 (rev. ed. 1968). His later poetry volumes include *The Dolphin* (1973), which won him a second Pulitzer Prize, and *Day by Day* (1977). His translations include *Phaedra* (1963) and *Prometheus Bound* (1969); *Imitations* (1961), free renderings of various European poets; and *The Voyage and Other Versions of Poems by Baudelaire* (1968). Lowell died in 1977.

In his poetry Lowell expressed the major tensions—both public and private—of his time with technical mastery and haunting authenticity. His earlier poems, dense with clashing images and discordant sounds, convey a view of the world whose bleakness is relieved by a religious mysticism compounded as much of doubt as of faith. Lowell's later poetry is composed in a more relaxed and conversational manner.

Another impressive formal poet was Theodore Roethke, who, influenced by William Butler Yeats, revealed a genius for ironic lyricism and a profound empathy for the processes of nature in *The Lost Son and Other Poems* (1948). Born in 1908, Roethke was educated at the University of Michigan (B.A., 1929; M.A., 1935) and Harvard University. He taught at several colleges and universities, notably the University of Washington, where he was a professor from 1947 until his death in 1963. His later career was interrupted by hospitalizations for bipolar disorder, but he nevertheless mentored a number of influential poets in his time at Washington, including Carolyn Kizer, James Wright, and David Wagoner.

Roethke had a number of his poems published in periodicals soon after finishing his undergraduate degree at the University of Michigan in 1929. His poetic style ranged from rigid, rhyming stanzas to ebullient free verse. His first book of poetry, *Open House*, which W.H. Auden called "completely successful," was published in 1941. It was followed by *The Lost Son and Other Poems* (1948) and *Praise to the End!* (1951). *The Waking: Poems 1933–1953* (1953) was awarded a Pulitzer Prize for poetry; *Words for the Wind* (1957) won a Bollingen Prize and a National Book Award. Roethke won a second National Book Award for *The Far*

Field (1964). His collected poems were published in 1966. His essays and lectures were collected in his *On the Poet and His Craft* (1965), and selections from his personal notebooks were published as *Straw for the Fire* (1972).

In addition to Lowell and Roethke, notable formal poets include the masterfully elegant Richard Wilbur (*Things of This World* [1956]); two war poets, Karl Shapiro (*V-Letter and Other Poems* [1944]) and Randall Jarrell (*Losses* [1948]); and a group of young poets influenced by W.H. Auden, including James Merrill, W.S. Merwin, James Wright, Adrienne Rich, and John Hollander. Although they displayed brilliant technical skill, they lacked Auden's strong personal voice.

EXPERIMENTATION AND BEAT POETRY

By the mid-1950s, however, a strong reaction had developed. Poets began to turn away from T.S. Eliot and Metaphysical poetry to more romantic or more prosaic models such as Walt Whitman, William Carlos Williams, Hart Crane, and D.H. Lawrence. A group of poets associated with Black Mountain College in western North Carolina, including Charles Olson, Robert Creeley, Robert Duncan, Edward Dorn, and Denise Levertov, treated the poem as an unfolding process rather than a containing form. Olson's *Maximus Poems* (1953–68) showed a clear affinity with the jagged line and uneven flow of Pound's *Cantos* and Williams's *Paterson*.

Allen Ginsberg's incantatory, prophetic *Howl* (1956) and his moving elegy for his mother, *Kaddish* (1961), gave powerful impetus to the Beat movement. Written with extraordinary intensity, these works were inspired by writers as diverse as Whitman, the biblical prophets, and

Black Mountain Poets

The Black Mountain poets were any of a loosely associated group of poets that formed an important part of the avant-garde of American poetry in the 1950s, publishing innovative yet disciplined verse in the *Black Mountain Review* (1954–57), which became a leading forum of experimental verse.

The group grew up around the poets Robert Creeley, Robert Duncan, and Charles Olson while they were teaching at Black Mountain College in North Carolina. Turning away from the poetic tradition espoused by T.S. Eliot, these poets emulated the freer style of William Carlos Williams. Charles Olson's essay "Projective Verse" (1950) became their manifesto. Olson emphasized the creative process, in which the poet's energy is transferred through the poem to the reader. Inherent in this new poetry was the reliance on decidedly American conversational language.

Much of the group's early work was published in the magazine *Origin* (1951–56). Dissatisfied with the lack of critical material in that magazine, Creeley and Olson established the Black Mountain Review. It featured the work of William Carlos Williams, Paul Blackburn, Denise Levertov, Allen Ginsberg, Gary Snyder, and many others who later became significant poets.

English poets William Blake and Christopher Smart, as well as by the dream logic of the French Surrealists and the spontaneous jazz aesthetic of Ginsberg's friend the novelist Jack Kerouac. Other noteworthy Beat poets included Lawrence Ferlinghetti, Gregory Corso, and Gary Snyder, a student of Eastern religion who, in *Turtle Island* (1974), continued the American tradition of nature poetry.

Ginsberg was born in 1926 and grew up in Paterson, N.J., where his father, Louis Ginsberg, himself a poet, taught English. Allen Ginsberg's mother, whom he mourned in his long poem *Kaddish* (1961), was confined for years in a mental hospital. Ginsberg was influenced in his work by the poet William Carlos Williams, particularly toward the use of natural speech rhythms and direct observations of unadorned actuality.

While at Columbia University, where his anarchical proclivities pained the authorities, Ginsberg became close friends with Jack Kerouac and William Burroughs, who were later numbered among the Beats. After leaving Columbia in 1948, he traveled widely and worked at a number of jobs from cafeteria floor mopper to market researcher.

Howl, Ginsberg's first published book, laments what he believed to have been the destruction by insanity of the "best minds of [his] generation." Dithyrambic and pro phetic, owing something to the romantic bohemianism of Walt Whitman, it also dwells on homosexuality, drug addiction, Buddhism, and Ginsberg's revulsion from what he saw as the materialism and insensitivity of post–World War II America.

Empty Mirror, a collection of earlier poems, appeared along with *Kaddish and Other Poems* in 1961, followed by *Reality Sandwiches* in 1963. *Kaddish,* one of Ginsberg's most important works, is a long confessional poem in which the poet laments his mother's insanity and tries to come to terms with both his relationship to her and with her death. In the early 1960s Ginsberg began a life of ceaseless travel, reading his poetry at campuses and coffee bars, traveling abroad, and engaging in left-wing political activities. He became an influential guru of the American youth coun terculture in the late 1960s. He acquired a deeper knowledge of Buddhism, and increasingly a religious ele ment of love for all sentient beings entered his work until his death in 1997.

His later volumes of poetry included *Planet News* (1968); *The Fall of America: Poems of These States, 1965–1971*

Allen Ginsberg's (left, with fellow poet W.H. Auden) first collection of poetry, the epic Howl, *became an inspiration for the Beat movement.* Evening Standard/Hulton Archive/Getty Images

(1972), which won the National Book Award; *Mind Breaths: Poems 1972–1977* (1978); and *White Shroud: Poems 1980–1985* (1986). His *Collected Poems 1947–1980* appeared in 1984. *Collected Poems, 1947–1997* (2006) is the first comprehensive one-volume collection of Ginsberg's published poetry. *The Letters of Allen Ginsberg* was published in 2008.

The openness of Beat poetry and the prosaic directness of Williams encouraged Lowell to develop a new autobiographical style in the laconic poetry and prose of *Life Studies* (1959) and *For the Union Dead* (1964). Lowell's new work influenced nearly all American poets but especially a group of "confessional" writers, including Anne

Lawrence Ferlinghetti

(b. March 24, 1919, Yonkers, N.Y.)

Poet Lawrence Ferlinghetti is best known as one of the founders of the Beat movement in San Francisco in the mid-1950s. His City Lights bookshop was an early gathering place of the Beats, and the publishing arm of City Lights was the first to print the Beats' books of poetry.

Ferlinghetti's father died shortly before Lawrence was born, his mother was placed in a mental hospital, and a female relative took him to France, where he spent most of his childhood. Later, they lived on a Long Island, N.Y., estate on which she was employed as a governess. He was a U.S. naval officer during World War II, and he received a B.A. at the University of North Carolina, an M.A. at Columbia University, and a doctorate at the Sorbonne in 1951.

In 1951 Ferlinghetti settled in San Francisco, and in 1953 he opened the City Lights Pocket Book Shop, which quickly became a gathering place for the city's literary avant garde. In 1955 Ferlinghetti's new City Lights press published his verse collection *Pictures of the Gone World,* which was the first paperback volume of the Pocket Poets series. Allen Ginsberg's *Howl and Other Poems* (1956) was originally published as the fourth volume in the series. City Lights Books printed other works by Ginsberg as well as books by Jack Kerouac, Gregory Corso, Denise Levertov, William Burroughs, William Carlos Williams, and foreign authors.

Ferlinghetti's own lucid, good-natured, witty verse was written in a conversational style and was designed to be read aloud. Popular in coffee houses and campus auditoriums, it struck a responsive chord in disaffected youth. His collection *A Coney Island of the Mind* (1958), with its notable verse "Autobiography," became the largest-selling book by any living American poet in the second half of the 20th century. The long poem *Tentative Description of a Dinner Given to Promote the Impeachment of President Eisenhower* (1958) was also popular. Ferlinghetti's later poems continued to be politically oriented, as suggested by such titles as *One Thousand Fearful Words for Fidel Castro* (1961), *Where Is Vietnam* (1965), *Tyrannus Nix?* (1969), and *Who Are We Now?* (1976). Retrospective collections of his poems were published as *Endless Life* (1981) and *These Are My Rivers* (1995). In 1988 Ferlinghetti published a short novel, *Love in the Days of Rage*, about a romance during the student revolution in France in 1968.

A Far Rockaway of the Heart, a sequel to *A Coney Island of the Mind*, appeared in 1997. In 1998 Ferlinghetti was named poet laureate of San Francisco, the first poet so honoured by the city. Two years later he published *What Is Poetry?*, a book of prose poetry, which was followed by the collection *How to Paint Sunlight* (2001) and *Americus: Part I* (2004), a history of the United States in verse.

Sexton in *To Bedlam and Part Way Back* (1960) and *All My Pretty Ones* (1962) and Sylvia Plath in the posthumously published *Ariel* (1965).

Sexton (née Anne Harvey) was born in 1928. She attended Garland Junior College for a year before her marriage in 1948 to Alfred M. Sexton II. She studied with Robert Lowell at Boston University and also worked as a model and a librarian. Although she had written some poetry in childhood, it was not until the later 1950s that she began to write seriously. Her poems, which showed Lowell's influence, appeared in *Harper's*, the *New Yorker*, *Partisan Review*, and other periodicals.

Her first book, *To Bedlam and Part Way Back*, was published in 1960. The book won immediate attention because of the intensely personal and relentlessly honest self-revelatory nature of the poems recording her nervous breakdown and recovery. Their imagery was frequently brilliant, and their tone was both sardonic and vulnerable. Her second book of poems, *All My Pretty Ones* (1962), continued in the vein of uncompromising self-exploration.

Live or Die (1966), a further record of emotional illness, won a Pulitzer Prize and was followed by, among others, *Love Poems* (1969), *Transformations* (1971), *The Book of Folly* (1972), and *The Death Notebooks* (1974).

Sexton taught at Boston University in 1970–71 and at Colgate University in 1971–72. She also wrote a number of children's books with poet Maxine Kumin, including *Eggs of Things* (1963), *Joey and the Birthday Present* (1971), and *The Wizard's Tears* (1975).

Sexton died by her own hand in 1974. *The Awful Rowing Toward God* (1975), *45 Mercy Street* (1976, edited by her daughter, Linda Gray Sexton), and *Uncollected Poems with Three Stories* (1978) were published posthumously. *Anne Sexton: A Self-Portrait in Letters*, edited by Lois Ames and Linda Gray Sexton, was published in 1977 and *No Evil Star: Selected Essays, Interviews, and Prose* in 1985.

Another Lowell-inspired confessional poet, Sylvia Plath, was born in 1932 and published her first poem at age eight. She entered and won many literary contests and while still in high school sold her first poem, to *Seventeen* magazine. She entered Smith College on a scholarship in 1951 and was a cowinner of the *Mademoiselle* magazine fiction contest in 1952. Despite her remarkable artistic, academic, and social success at Smith, Plath suffered from severe depression and underwent a period of psychiatric hospitalization. She graduated from Smith with highest honours in 1955 and went on to Newnham College in Cambridge, Eng., on a Fulbright fellowship. In 1956 she married the English poet Ted Hughes. For the following two years she was an instructor in English at Smith College.

In 1960, shortly after Plath and her husband returned to England, her first collection of poems appeared as *The Colossus*. Her second book, a strongly autobiographical novel titled *The Bell Jar*, was published in 1963 under the pseudonym "Victoria Lucas." The book describes the mental breakdown, attempted suicide, and eventual recovery of a young college girl.

During her last three years Plath abandoned the restraints and conventions that had bound much of her early work. She wrote with great speed, producing poems of stark self-revelation and confession. The anxiety, confusion, and doubt that haunted her were transmuted into verses of great power and pathos borne on flashes of incisive wit. In 1963, after a burst of productivity, Plath took her own life.

Ariel (1965), a collection of her later poems, helped spark the growth of something of a cult devoted to Plath. The reissue of *The Bell Jar* under her own name in 1966 and the appearance of small collections of previously unpublished poems, including *Crossing the Water* (1971) and *Winter Trees* (1971), were welcomed by critics and the public alike. *Johnny Panic and the Bible of Dreams*, a book of short stories and prose, was published in 1977, and *The Collected Poems*, which includes many previously unpublished poems, appeared in 1981. Plath had kept a journal for much of her life, and in 2000 *The Unabridged Journals of Sylvia Plath*, covering the years from 1950 to 1962, was published. A biographical film of Plath starring Gwyneth Paltrow (*Sylvia*) appeared in 2003. In 2009 Plath's radio play *Three Women* (1962) was staged professionally for the first time.

Another poet influenced by Lowell was John Berryman, whose *Dream Songs* (1964, 1968) combined autobiographical fragments with minstrel-show motifs to create a zany style of self-projection and comic-tragic lament. Born in 1914, Berryman was brought up a strict Roman Catholic in the small Oklahoma town of Anadarko, moving at 10 with his family to Tampa, Fla. When the boy was 12, his father killed himself. Berryman attended a private school in Connecticut and graduated from Columbia University, where he was influenced by his teacher, the poet Mark Van Doren. After study at the University of Cambridge in 1938, he returned to the United States to teach at Wayne State University, Detroit, beginning a career that included posts at Harvard, Princeton, and the University of Minnesota.

He began to publish in little magazines during the late 1930s, and in 1940 *Five Young American Poets* contained 20 of his poems. Two other volumes of poetry—*Poems* (1942) and *The Dispossessed* (1948)—followed. A richly erotic autobiographical sequence about a love affair, *Berryman's Sonnets,* appeared in 1967. Berryman was a versatile man of letters: "The Lovers" appeared in *The Best American Short Stories of 1946,* and his story "The Imaginary Jew" (1945) is often anthologized. His biography of Stephen Crane was published in 1950.

Homage to Mistress Bradstreet is a monologue that pays tribute to Anne Bradstreet, the first American woman poet: Sometimes her voice is heard, sometimes Berryman's, and throughout a loving and intimate grasp of the details of American history is manifest. His new technical daring was also evident in *77 Dream Songs* (1964), augmented to form a sequence of 385 "Dream Songs" by *His Toy, His Dream, His Rest* (1968). Berryman's work bears some relation to the "confessional" school of poetry that flourished among many of his contemporaries, but in his case bursts of humour sporadically light up the troubled interior landscape. This autobiographical note continued to be sounded in *Love & Fame* (1970), in which he conveys much in a deceptively offhand manner.

Berryman committed suicide in 1972 by jumping from a bridge onto the ice of the Mississippi River. *Recovery,* an account of his struggle against alcoholism, was published in 1973.

DEEP IMAGE POETS

Through his personal charisma and his magazine *The Fifties* (later *The Sixties* and *The Seventies*), Robert Bly encouraged a number of poets to shift their work toward the individual voice and open form: Galway Kinnell, James Wright, David Ignatow, and, less directly, Louis Simpson, James Dickey, and Donald Hall. Sometimes called the "deep image" poets, Bly and his friends sought spiritual intensity and transcendence of the self rather than confessional immediacy. Their work was influenced by the poetry of Spanish and Latin American writers such as Federico García Lorca, Juan Ramón Jiménez, César Vallejo, and Pablo Neruda, especially their surreal association of images, as well as by the "greenhouse poems" (1946–48) and the later meditative poetry of Roethke, with their deep feeling for nature as a vehicle of spiritual transformation. Yet, like their Hispanic models, they were also political poets, instrumental in organizing protest and writing poems against the Vietnam War. Kinnell was a Lawrentian poet who, in poems such as "The Porcupine" and "The Bear," gave the brutality of nature the power of myth. His vatic sequence, *The Book of Nightmares* (1971), and the quieter poems in *Mortal Acts, Mortal Words* (1980) are among the most rhetorically effective works in contemporary poetry.

Although his influence on the school of "deep image" poets was great, Bly was a noted poet, translator, editor, and author. He is perhaps best known to the public at large as the author of *Iron John: A Book About Men* (1990; reprinted 2001 as *Iron John: Men and Masculinity*). Drawing on Jungian psychology, myth, legend, folklore, and fairy tales (the title is taken from a story by the Grimm Brothers), the book demonstrates Bly's masculinist convictions. It had many detractors, but it proved an important, creative, and best-selling work on the subject of manhood and masculinity for a budding men's movement in the United States.

Bly was born in 1926 and grew up on a farm in rural Minnesota. After serving in the U.S. Navy, Bly studied at St. Olaf College in Northfield, Minn. (1946–47), Harvard University (B.A., 1950), and the University of Iowa (M.A., 1956). In 1958 he cofounded *The Fifties*, which published translations and poetry by Bly and other important young poets. Bly's first collection of poems, *Silence in the Snowy Fields* (1962), reveals his sense of man in nature. It was followed by *The Light Around the Body* (1968), which won a National Book Award.

Further volumes of poems and prose poems include *Sleepers Joining Hands* (1973), *This Body Is Made of Camphor and Gopherwood* (1977), *This Tree Will Be Here for a Thousand Years* (1979), *Morning Poems* (1997), and *Eating the Honey of Words* (1999). His poems in *The Man in the Black Coat Turns* (1981) explore themes of male grief and the father–son connection that he developed further in *Iron John* and also *The Maiden King: The Reunion of Masculine and Feminine* (1999), written with Marion Woodman.

A collection of Bly's prose poems appeared in 1992 under the title *What Have I Ever Lost by Dying?* Such later collections as *Meditations on the Insatiable Soul* (1994) and *The Urge to Travel Long Distances* (2005) are preoccupied with the pastoral landscape of Minnesota. Bly employed the Arabic *ghazal* form in the poems comprising *The Night Abraham Called to the Stars* (2001) and *My Sentence Was a Thousand Years of Joy* (2005). He also released a volume of poems protesting the Iraq War, *The Insanity of Empire* (2004). Bly dubbed the poems in *Turkish Pears in August* (2007) "ramages," referencing *rameau*, the French word for branch. They each contain 85 syllables and focus on a certain vowel sound.

James Dickey

(b. Feb. 2, 1923, Atlanta, Ga.—d. Jan. 19, 1997, Columbia, S.C.)

James Dickey was a poet, novelist, and critic best known for his poetry combining themes of nature mysticism, religion, and history and for his novel *Deliverance* (1970).

Dickey attended Clemson College in South Carolina before serving as a fighter-bomber pilot in the U.S. Army Air Forces during World War II, flying dozens of missions in the South Pacific. After the war he earned B.A. (1949) and M.A. (1950) degrees from Vanderbilt University in Nashville, Tenn. He reentered military service as an Air Force training officer during the Korean War.

By his own account, Dickey began writing poetry at the age of 24 years with little awareness of formal poetics. After pursuing graduate studies and working for a time in advertising ("selling [his] soul to the devil in the daytime and buying it back at night," as he put it), he published his first book of poems, *Into the Stone*, in 1960. He was a teacher and writer-in-residence at a number of American universities and colleges, including the University of South Carolina (from 1968). From 1966 to 1968 he served as poetry consultant to the Library of Congress (now poet laureate consultant in poetry). Dickey's poetry is noted for its lyrical portrayal of a world in conflict—predator with prey, soldier with soldier, the self with itself.

Dickey's other collections of poetry include *Drowning with Others* (1962), *Helmets* (1964), *Buckdancer's Choice* (1965), *Poems 1957–1967* (1967), *The Zodiac* (1976), *The Whole Motion* (1992; collected poems, 1949–92), and *Selected Poems* (1998). Of his works of nonfiction prose, *Babel to Byzantium: Poets & Poetry Now* (1968), the autobiographical *Self-Interviews* (1970), and *Jericho: The South Beheld* (1974) are notable. His best-known novel, *Deliverance*, is a harrowing account of a disastrous canoe trip four men take down a Georgia river. A highly successful film version of the novel was produced from Dickey's own screenplay in 1972. A later adventure novel, *To the White Sea* (1993), also was popular. His early notebooks were published as *Striking In* (1996).

Bly translated the work of many poets, ranging from Rainer Maria Rilke (German) and Tomas Tranströmer (Swedish) to Pablo Neruda and Antonio Machado (Spanish). Additionally, he translated several works from Norwegian, including Knut Hamsun's novel *Hunger* (1890; translated 1967) and Henrik Ibsen's play *Peer Gynt* (1867; translated 2008). He also reworked English translations of poetry by the Indian mystic Kabir (translated from Bengali by Rabindranath Tagore) and the Indian poet Mīrzā Asadullāh Khān Ghālib (translated from Urdu by Sunil Datta). Bly was named poet laureate of Minnesota in 2008.

NEW DIRECTIONS

James Wright's style changed dramatically in the early 1960s. He abandoned his stiffly formal verse for the stripped-down, meditative lyricism of *The Branch Will Not Break* (1963) and *Shall We Gather at the River* (1968), which were more dependent on the emotional tenor of image than on metre, poetic diction, or rhyme. In books such as *Figures of the Human* (1964) and *Rescue the Dead* (1968), David Ignatow wrote brief but razor-sharp poems that made their effect through swiftness, deceptive simplicity, paradox, and personal immediacy. Another poet whose work ran the gamut from prosaic simplicity to Emersonian transcendence was A.R. Ammons. His short poems in *Briefings* (1971) were close to autobiographical jottings, small glimpses, and observations, but, like his longer poems, they turned the natural world into a source of vision. Like Ignatow, he made it a virtue to seem unliterary and found illumination in the pedestrian and the ordinary.

Both daily life and an exposure to French Surrealism helped inspire a group of New York poets, among them

Poetic Diction

Poetic diction is grandiose, elevated, and unfamiliar language, supposedly the prerogative of poetry but not of prose. The earliest critical reference to poetic diction is Aristotle's remark in the *Poetics* that it should be clear without being "mean." But subsequent generations of poets were more scrupulous in avoiding meanness than in cultivating clarity. Depending heavily on expressions used by previous poets, they evolved in time a language sprinkled with such archaic terms as "eftsoons," "prithee," "oft," and "ere." It was this "inane phraseology" that William Wordsworth rebelled against in his preface to the *Lyrical Ballads* (1800), in which he advocated a poetry written in the "language really used by men." Subsequent critics, notably Samuel Taylor Coleridge in *Biographia Literaria* (1817), felt that Wordsworth overstated the case, that his own best work contradicted his theory, and that some of his work written in "the language really used by men" did not achieve the level of poetry.

Modern critics take the position that there is no diction peculiar to poetry, but there may be a diction peculiar to an individual poem. Thus, Shakespeare's sonnet "Not marble, nor the gilded monuments," beginning with such images of stately dignity, continues with words evocative of public pomp and temporal power.

Frank O'Hara. Whether O'Hara was jotting down a sequence of ordinary moments or paying tribute to film stars, his poems had a breathless immediacy that was distinctive and unique.

Born in 1926 and raised in central Massachusetts, O'Hara was drawn to both poetry and the visual arts for much of his life. He studied at Harvard University (B.A., 1950) and the University of Michigan (M.A., 1951). During the 1960s, as an assistant curator at the Museum of Modern Art in New York City, O'Hara sent his fine criticism of current painting and sculpture to such periodicals as *Art*

Inspired by French surrealist works, Frank O'Hara created poems from snippets from all walks of life, at times collaborating with visual artists for "poem-paintings." John Jonas Gruen/Hulton Archive/Getty Images

News, and he wrote catalogs for exhibits that he arranged. Meanwhile, local theatres were producing many of his experimental one-act plays, including *Try! Try!* (1960), about a soldier's return to his wife and her new lover.

O'Hara, however, considered himself primarily a poet. His pieces are a mixture of quotations, gossip, phone numbers, commercials—any mote of experience that he found appealing. O'Hara also drew inspiration from non-literary sources, including free-form jazz and the abstract paintings of acquaintances such as Jackson Pollock and Larry Rivers, whose work he championed in art criticism. (His interest in both poetry and visual art came together with a series of "poem-paintings" he produced in collaboration with the artist Norman Bluhm in 1960.) The results vary from the merely idiosyncratic to the dynamic and humorous. His reputation grew in the 1960s to the point that he was considered one of the most important and influential postwar American poets at the time of his death, in 1966 at age 40, after being hit by a car while on vacation.

O'Hara's first volume of poetry was *A City Winter and Other Poems* (1952). His most celebrated collections are *Meditations in an Emergency* (1957) and *Lunch Poems* (1964). *The Collected Poems of Frank O'Hara* (1971) and its successor, *Selected Poems* (2008), were published posthumously.

Three other notable poets of the New York school were Kenneth Koch, James Schuyler, and John Ashbery. Koch's comic voice swung effortlessly from the trivial to the fantastic. Schuyler was an acute observer of natural landscapes who described common experiences with familiar images in compact lines of varied rhythm. Strongly influenced by Wallace Stevens, Ashbery's ruminative poems can seem random, discursive, and enigmatic. Avoiding poetic colour, they do their work by suggestion and association, exploring the interface between experience and perception.

Other impressive poets of the postwar years included Elizabeth Bishop, whose precise, loving attention to objects was reminiscent of her early mentor, Marianne Moore. Although she avoided the confessional mode of her friend Lowell, her sense of place, her heartbreaking decorum, and her keen powers of observation gave her work a strong personal cast.

Bishop was born in 1911 and reared by her maternal grandparents in Nova Scotia and by an aunt in Boston. After graduating from Vassar College in 1934, she often traveled abroad, living for a time in Key West, Fla. (1938–42), and Mexico (1943). She was consultant in poetry at the Library of Congress (now poet laureate consultant in poetry) from 1949 to 1950. During most of the 1950s and '60s she lived with Lota de Macedo Soares in Petrópolis, Braz., near Rio de Janeiro, later dividing the year between Petrópolis and San Francisco. Her first book of poems, *North & South* (1946), captures the divided nature of Bishop's allegiances: born in New England and reared there and in Nova Scotia, she eventually migrated to hotter regions. This book was reprinted in 1955, with additions, as *North & South: A Cold Spring*, and it won a Pulitzer Prize.

Much of Bishop's later work also addresses the frigid-tropical dichotomy of a New England conscience in a tropical sphere. *Questions of Travel* (1965) and *Geography III* (1976) offer spare, powerful meditations on the need for self-exploration, on the value of art (especially poetry) in human life, and on human responsibility in a chaotic world. The latter collection includes some of Bishop's best-known poems, among them "In the Waiting Room," "Crusoe in England," and the exquisite villanelle "One Art." A collection entitled *The Complete Poems* was published in 1969.

Bishop taught writing at Harvard University from 1970 to 1977, and she was elected to the American Academy of Arts and Letters in 1976. Her posthumously published poetry collections (she died in 1979) include *The Complete Poems, 1927–1979* (1983) and *Edgar Allen Poe & the Juke-Box* (2006), the latter of which contains previously unpublished material. *The Collected Prose*, a volume of fiction and nonfiction, appeared in 1984. A selection of her letters was published under the title *One Art* in 1994. *Elizabeth Bishop: Poems, Prose, and Letters* (2008) is a comprehensive collection of her published and unpublished work.

Bishop also wrote a travel book, *Brazil* (1962), and translated from the Portuguese Alice Brant's Brazilian classic, *The Diary of Helena Morley* (1957). She edited and translated *An Anthology of Twentieth-Century Brazilian Poetry* (1972). Bishop also was an artist, and *Exchanging Hats* (1996) is a collection of more than 50 of her paintings.

In *The Changing Light at Sandover* (1982), James Merrill, previously a polished lyric poet, made his mandarin style the vehicle of a lighthearted personal epic, in which he, with the help of a Ouija board, called up the shades of all his dead friends, including the poet Auden.

Merrill was born in 1926, the son of Charles E. Merrill, a founder of Merrill Lynch, an investment-banking firm. He attended private schools and Amherst College (B.A., 1947), and inherited wealth enabled him to devote his life to his poetry. The novelist Alison Lurie, who was a friend, described him as "a kind of Martian: supernaturally brilliant, detached, quizzical, apart" in her biography of Merrill and his longtime companion, David Jackson.

Merrill's first book, *First Poems* (1951), and subsequent collections revealed his formal mastery but were somewhat impersonal and artificial in tone. With *Water Street* (1962), critics noted a growing ease and the development of a personal vision in his writing. With *Nights and Days* (1966), which won the National Book Award in Poetry, *The Fire Screen* (1969), and *Braving the Elements* (1972), Merrill gained wider public appreciation. His verse in these books was more autobiographical and tended to focus on poignant moments in his romantic and domestic life. He skillfully combined lyric language with ordinary conversation and

At times James Merrill was known to seek inspiration from his Ouija board for his formal yet witty poetry. ©AP Images

possessed a voice that could be witty, intimate, and collo-quial while retaining a high degree of formal elegance.

The publication of the epic poetry in the Pulitzer Prize-winning *Divine Comedies* (1976), *Mirabell: Books of Number* (1978), for which he won a second National Book Award, and *Scripts for the Pageant* (1980)—a trilogy later published in *The Changing Light at Sandover* (1982)—established Merrill as one of the leading American poets of

147

his generation. This 17,000-line work presents a series of conversations held with various real and fictional persons in the spirit world by means of a Ouija board, a device that enabled Merrill to compose a serious yet witty summation of his lifelong concerns. A selection of his poetry, *From the First Nine: Poems 1946–1976*, was published in 1982. The poetry collection *The Inner Room* (1988) won the Library of Congress's first Bobbitt National Prize for Poetry. Merrill also wrote plays, novels, essays, and the memoir *A Different Person* (1993). His 15th and last book of poetry, *A Scattering of Salts*, appeared soon after his death in 1995. His *Collected Poems* was published in 2001. One critic spoke of the "lapidary smoothness and mosaic fit," reminiscent of the Roman poet Horace, that marked Merrill's poetry.

Archibald MacLeish

(b. May 7, 1892, Glencoe, Ill.—d. April 20, 1982, Boston, Mass.)

Archibald MacLeish was a poet, playwright, teacher, and public official, whose concern for liberal democracy figured in much of his work. However, his most memorable lyrics are of a more private nature.

MacLeish attended Yale University, where he was active in literature and football. He graduated in 1915 and then earned a law degree at Harvard. While there, he married Ada Hitchcock of Connecticut, a union that lasted for the rest of his life.

After three years as an attorney in Boston, MacLeish went to France in 1923 to perfect his poetic craft. The verse he published during his expatriate years—*The Happy Marriage* (1924), *The Pot of Earth* (1925), *Streets in the Moon* (1926), and *The Hamlet of A. MacLeish* (1928)—shows the fashionable influence of Ezra Pound and T.S. Eliot. During this period he wrote his much-anthologized poem "Ars Poetica" (1926). After returning to the United States in 1928, he published *New Found Land*

(1930), which reveals the simple lyric eloquence that is the persistent MacLeish note. It includes one of his most frequently anthologized poems, "You, Andrew Marvell."

In the 1930s MacLeish became increasingly concerned about the menace of fascism. *Conquistador* (1932, Pulitzer Prize), about the conquest and exploitation of Mexico, was the first of his "public" poems. Other poems were collected in *Frescoes for Mr. Rockefeller's City* (1933), *Public Speech* (1936), and *America Was Promises* (1939). His *Collected Poems 1917–1952* (1952) was awarded a Pulitzer Prize. His radio verse plays include *The Fall of the City* (1937), *Air Raid* (1938), and *The Great American Fourth of July Parade* (1975).

MacLeish served as librarian of Congress (1939–44) and assistant secretary of state (1944–45) and in various other governmental positions until 1949, when he became Boylston professor at Harvard, where he remained until 1962. His verse drama *J.B.*, based on the biblical story of Job, was performed on Broadway in 1958 and won MacLeish his third Pulitzer Prize. *A Continuing Journey* (1968) and *Riders on the Earth* (1978) are collections of essays. *Collected Poems 1917–1982* (1985) was published posthumously.

In a prolific career highlighted by such poems as *Reflections on Espionage* (1976), "Blue Wine" (1979), and *Powers of Thirteen* (1983), John Hollander, like Merrill, displayed enormous technical virtuosity. Richard Howard imagined witty monologues and dialogues for famous people of the past in poems collected in *Untitled Subjects* (1969) and *Two-Part Inventions* (1974).

AUTOBIOGRAPHICAL APPROACHES

With the autobiographical knots and parables of *Reasons for Moving* (1968) and *Darker* (1970), Mark Strand's paradoxical language achieved a resonant simplicity. He enhanced his reputation with *Dark Harbor* (1993) and

Blizzard of One (1998). Other strongly autobiographical poets working with subtle technique and intelligence in a variety of forms included Philip Levine, Charles Simic, Robert Pinsky, Gerald Stern, Louise Glück, and Sharon Olds. Levine's background in working class Detroit gave his work a unique cast, while Glück and Olds brought a terrific emotional intensity to their poems. Pinsky's poems were collected in *The Figured Wheel* (1996). He became a tireless and effective advocate for poetry during his tenure as poet laureate from 1997 to 2000. With the sinuous sentences and long flowing lines of *Tar* (1983) and *Flesh and Blood* (1987), C.K. Williams perfected a narrative technique founded on distinctive voice, sharply etched emotion, and cleanly observed detail. He received the Pulitzer Prize for *Repair* (2000).

Adrienne Rich's work gained a burning immediacy from her lesbian feminism. *The Will to Change* (1971) and *Diving into the Wreck* (1973) were turning points for women's poetry in the wake of the 1960s.

Rich was born in 1929. She attended Radcliffe College (B.A., 1951), and before her graduation her poetry was chosen by W.H. Auden for publication in the Yale Younger Poets series. The resulting volume, *A Change of World* (1951), reflected her mastery of the formal elements of poetry and her considerable restraint. *The Diamond Cutters and Other Poems* (1955) was followed by *Snapshots of a Daughter-in-Law: Poems 1954–1962* (1963), published long after her earlier volumes. This third collection exhibited a change in style, a movement away from the restrained and formal to a looser, more personal form. In the mid-1950s Rich began to date her poems to give them a historical context. Her fourth volume, *Necessities of Life: Poems 1962–1965* (1966), was written almost entirely in free verse.

In 1966 Rich separated from her husband (who committed suicide in 1970). She moved in with her partner,

Constantly experimenting with form and voice, feminist poet and literary critic Adrienne Rich wrote works that became pivotal for women's writing after the 1960s. Nancy R. Schiff/Hulton Archive/Getty Images

novelist Michelle Cliff, in 1976. Throughout the 1960s and '70s, Rich's increasing commitment to the women's movement and to a lesbian and feminist aesthetic politicized much of her poetry. *Leaflets: Poems 1965–1968* (1969) includes a number of translations of poetry from other languages as well as a series of poems echoing the Middle Eastern *ghazal* genre. Such collections as *Diving into the Wreck: Poems 1971–1972* (1973; National Book Award) and *The Dream of a Common Language: Poems 1974–1977* (1978) express anger at the societal conception of womanhood and further articulate Rich's lesbian identity. Her later volumes, *A Wild Patience Has Taken Me This Far: Poems 1978–1981* (1981), *An Atlas of the Difficult World: Poems 1988–1991* (1991), and *Dark Fields of the Republic: Poems 1991–1995* (1995), pay tribute to early feminists and admonish the reader to recall the lessons of history, often through the use of different voices.

In such later collections as *Midnight Salvage: Poems 1995–1998* (1999), *Fox: Poems 1998–2000* (2001), and *The School Among the Ruins: Poems 2000–2004* (2004), Rich turned her gaze to social problems as diverse as cell phone usage and the Iraq War, using forms more elliptical and fragmented than those present in her earlier work. The poems in *Telephone Ringing in the Labyrinth* (2007) continue to experiment with form and include more reflective passages on age and dying with Rich's sharp observations on the cultural climate of the day. Selections from her body of work were published in *Collected Early Poems 1950–1970* (1993) and *Selected Poems 1950–1995* (1996).

Rich also wrote several books of criticism. *Of Woman Born: Motherhood as Experience and Institution* (1976) combines scholarly research with personal reflections on being a mother, whereas *On Lies, Secrets, and Silence* (1979) traces history through musings on Rich's own various incarnations. In *Blood, Bread, and Poetry* (1986), *What Is Found There: Notebooks on Poetry and Politics* (1993), and *Arts of the Possible: Essays and Conversations* (2001), Rich addressed many of the problems plaguing humanity, as well as the role of her art form in addressing them.

Rich turned down the National Medal of the Arts in 1997, publicly claiming that the politics of the Bill Clinton administration conflicted with her ideas about art. She was awarded the Bollingen Prize in 2003. Rich taught at numerous universities across the United States, including Stanford and Cornell.

The 1960s also enabled some older poets to become more loosely autobiographical and freshly imaginative, among them Stanley Kunitz, Robert Penn Warren, and

Gwendolyn Brooks

(b. June 7, 1917, Topeka, Kan.—d. Dec. 3, 2000, Chicago, Ill.)

Gwendolyn Brooks was a poet whose works deal with the everyday life of urban blacks. She was the first African American poet to win the Pulitzer Prize (1949), and in 1968 she was named the poet laureate of Illinois.

Gwendolyn Brooks became the first African American to win the Pulitzer Prize for poetry. Her work often featured the daily life of urban blacks. Slim Aarons/Hulton Archive/Getty Images

Brooks graduated from Wilson Junior College in Chicago in 1936. Her early verses appeared in the *Chicago Defender*, a newspaper written primarily for that city's African American community. Her first published collection, *A Street in Bronzeville* (1945), reveals her talent for making the ordinary life of her neighbours extraordinary. *Annie Allen* (1949), for which she won the Pulitzer Prize, is a loosely connected series of poems related to an African American girl's growing up in Chicago. The same theme was used for Brooks's novel, *Maud Martha* (1953).

The Bean Eaters (1960) contains some of her best verse. Her *Selected Poems* (1963) was followed in 1968 by *In the Mecca*, half of which is a long narrative poem about people in the Mecca, a vast, fortresslike apartment building erected on the South Side of Chicago in 1891, which had long since deteriorated into a slum. The second half of the book contains individual poems, among which the most noteworthy are "Boy Breaking Glass" and "Malcolm X." Brooks also wrote a book for children, *Bronzeville Boys and Girls* (1956). The autobiographical *Report from Part One* (1972) was an assemblage of personal memoirs, interviews, and letters, which was followed, though much later, by *Report from Part Two* (1996). Her other works include *Primer for Blacks* (1980), *Young Poet's Primer* (1980), *To Disembark* (1981), *The Near-Johannesburg Boy, and Other Poems* (1986), *Blacks* (1987), *Winnie* (1988), and *Children Coming Home* (1991).

In 1985–86 Brooks was Library of Congress consultant in poetry (now poet laureate consultant in poetry), and in 1989 she received a lifetime achievement award from the National Endowment for the Arts. She became a professor of English at Chicago State University in 1990, a position she held until her death.

W.S. Merwin. The decade invigorated gifted black poets such as Robert Hayden, Gwendolyn Brooks, and Michael S. Harper. It formed the background for the work of the young poets of the 1980s, such as Edward Hirsch, Alan Shapiro, Jorie Graham, Cathy Song, and Rita Dove, whose sequence about her grandparents, *Thomas and Beulah*, was awarded the Pulitzer Prize in 1987. Graham's increasingly abstract and elusive work culminated in *The Dream of the Unified Field* (1995), selected from five previous volumes. The AIDS crisis inspired *My Alexandria* (1993) by Mark Doty, *The Man with Night Sweats* (1992) by Thom Gunn, and a superb memoir, *Borrowed Time* (1988), and a cycle of poems, *Love Alone* (1988), by the poet Paul Monette. With razor-sharp images and finely honed descriptive touches, Louisiana-born Yusef Komunyakaa emerged as an impressive African American voice in the 1990s. He wrote about his time as a soldier and war correspondent in Vietnam in *Dien Cai Dau* (1988) and received the Pulitzer Prize in 1994 for his volume of new and selected poems *Neon Vernacular* (1993). His poems were collected in *Pleasure Dome* (2001). Billy Collins found a huge audience for his engagingly witty and conversational poetry, especially that collected in *Sailing Alone Around the Room* (2001), published the year he became poet laureate.

CHAPTER 4

POSTWAR AMERICAN DRAMA

Although American drama reached its peak in the early 20th-century plays of Eugene O'Neill, three post–World War II playwrights established reputations nearly comparable to O'Neill's.

MILLER, WILLIAMS, AND ALBEE

Arthur Miller wrote eloquent essays defending his modern, democratic concept of tragedy. Despite its abstract, allegorical quality and portentous language, *Death of a Salesman* (1949) came close to vindicating his views. Miller's intense family dramas were rooted in the problem dramas of Henrik Ibsen and the works of the socially conscious ethnic dramatists of the 1930s, especially Clifford Odets, but Miller gave them a metaphysical turn. From *All My Sons* (1947) to *The Price* (1968), his work was at its strongest when he dealt with father-son relationships, anchored in the harsh realities of the Great Depression. Yet Miller could also be an effective protest writer, as in *The Crucible* (1953), which used the Salem witch trials to attack the witch-hunting of the McCarthy era.

Although his work was uneven, Tennessee Williams at his best was a more powerful and effective playwright than Miller. Creating stellar roles for actors, especially women, Williams brought a passionate lyricism and a tragic

Salem Witch Trials

In American history, the Salem witch trials were a series of investigations and persecutions that took place between May and October of 1692, which caused 19 convicted "witches" to be hanged and many other suspects to be imprisoned in the town of Salem in the Massachusetts Bay Colony. Stimulated by voodoo tales told by a West Indian slave, Tituba, a few young girls claimed they were possessed by the devil and subsequently accused three Salem women, including Tituba, of witchcraft. As Tituba and other accused persons were pressured and consequently incriminated others in false confessions, public hysteria over the threat of witchcraft mounted throughout Massachusetts.

Civil magistrates, encouraged by the clergy, set up a special court in Salem to try those accused of practicing witchcraft, and Samuel Sewall, John Hathorne, and William Stoughton were chosen as the court's judges. The list of the accused increased (even Massachusetts governor William Phips's wife was implicated) until 150 people had been imprisoned and were awaiting trial. By September, however, the climate of mass hysteria had begun to abate, and public opinion first stopped, and then condemned, the trials. Governor Phips dissolved the special court in October and released the remaining prisoners. The Massachusetts General Court (legislature) later annulled the witch trials' convictions and granted indemnities to the families of those who had been executed.

Southern vision to such plays as *The Glass Menagerie* (1944), *A Streetcar Named Desire* (1947), *Cat on a Hot Tin Roof* (1955), and *The Night of the Iguana* (1961). He empathized with his characters' dreams and illusions and with the frustrations and defeats of their lives, and he wrote about his own dreams and disappointments in his beautifully etched short fiction, from which his plays were often adapted.

A scene from a 1955 production of Arthur Miller's The Crucible. *The play used the Salem witchcraft trials as an allegory for a U.S. Congressional investigation into allegedly subversive activities during the 1950s.* Thurston Hopkins/Hulton Archive/Getty Images

Miller and Williams dominated the post–World War II theatre until the 1960s, and few other playwrights emerged to challenge them. Then, in 1962, Edward Albee's reputation, based on short plays such as *The Zoo Story* (1959) and *The American Dream* (1960), was secured by the stunning power of *Who's Afraid of Virginia Woolf?* A master of absurdist theatre who assimilated the influence of European playwrights such as Samuel Beckett and Eugène Ionesco, Albee established himself as a major figure in American drama. His reputation with critics and audiences, however, began to decline with enigmatic plays such as *Tiny Alice* (1964) and *A Delicate Balance* (1966), but, like O'Neill, he eventually returned to favour with a complex autobiographical drama, *Three Tall Women* (1994).

ARTHUR MILLER

(b. Oct. 17, 1915, New York, N.Y.—d. Feb. 10, 2005, Roxbury, Conn.)

Arthur Miller was an American playwright, who combined social awareness with a searching concern for his characters' inner lives. He is best known for *Death of a Salesman* (1949).

Although his short stories and plays featured an acute social awareness, Arthur Miller also is noted for delving into the inner lives of his characters. Charles Hewitt/Hulton Archive/Getty Images

Miller was shaped by the Great Depression, which spelled financial ruin for his father, a small manufacturer, and demonstrated to the young Miller the insecurity of modern existence. After graduation from high school he worked in a warehouse. With the money he earned he attended the University of Michigan (B.A., 1938), where he began to write plays. His first public success was with *Focus* (1945), a novel about anti-Semitism. *All My Sons* (1947), a drama about a manufacturer of faulty war materials that strongly reflects the influence of Henrik Ibsen, was his first important play. *Death of a Salesman* became one of the most famous American plays of its period. It is the tragedy of Willy Loman, a small man destroyed by false values that are in large part the values of his society. Miller received a Pulitzer Prize for the play, which was later adapted for the screen (1951).

The Crucible (1953) was based on the witchcraft trials in Salem, Mass., in 1692, a period Miller considered relevant to the 1950s, when investigation of subversive activities was widespread. In 1956, when Miller was called before the House Un-American Activities Committee, he refused to name people he had seen 10 years earlier at an alleged communist writers' meeting. He was convicted of contempt but appealed and won.

A Memory of Two Mondays and another short play, *A View from the Bridge* (a story of an Italian-American longshoreman whose passion for his niece destroys him), were staged on the same bill in 1955. *After the Fall* (1964) is concerned with failure in human relationships and its consequences. *The Price* (1968) continued Miller's exploration of the theme of guilt and responsibility to oneself and to others by examining the strained relationship between two brothers. He directed the London production of the play in 1969. *The Archbishop's Ceiling*, produced in Washington, D.C., in 1977, dealt with the Soviet treatment of dissident writers. *The American Clock*, a series of dramatic vignettes based on Studs Terkel's *Hard Times* (about the Great Depression), was produced at the 1980 American Spoleto Festival in Charleston, S.C. Later plays include *The Ride Down Mount Morgan* (1991), *Mr. Peters' Connections* (1998), and *Resurrection Blues* (2002).

Miller also wrote a screenplay, *The Misfits* (1961), for his second wife, the actress Marilyn Monroe (1926–62); they were married from 1956 to 1961. The filming of *The Misfits* served as the basis for the play *Finishing the Picture* (2004). *I Don't Need You Any More*, a collection of his short stories, appeared in 1967 and a collection of theatre essays in 1977. His autobiography, *Timebends*, was published in 1987.

TENNESSEE WILLIAMS

(b. March 26, 1911, Columbus, Miss.—d. Feb. 25, 1983, New York, N.Y.)

Tennessee Williams was a dramatist whose plays reveal a world of human frustration in which sex and violence underlie an atmosphere of romantic gentility. Born in the Deep South, Thomas Lanier Williams moved with his family to St. Louis in 1918. He became interested in playwriting while at the University of Missouri (Columbia) and Washington University (St. Louis) and worked at it even during the Depression while employed in a St. Louis shoe factory. (While in college, he earned the nickname "Tennessee" because of his pronounced Southern accent.) Little theatre groups produced some of his work, encouraging him to study dramatic writing at the University of Iowa, where he earned a B.A. in 1938.

His first recognition came when *American Blues* (1939), a group of one-act plays, won a Group Theatre award. Williams, however, continued to work at jobs ranging from theatre usher to Hollywood scriptwriter until

Tennessee Williams. Encyclopædia Britannica, Inc.

success came with *The Glass Menagerie* (1944). In it, Williams portrayed a declassed Southern family living in a tenement. The play is about the failure of a domineering mother, Amanda, living upon her delusions of a romantic past, and her cynical son, Tom, to secure a suitor for Tom's crippled and painfully shy sister, Laura, who lives in a fantasy world with a collection of glass animals.

Williams's next major play, *A Streetcar Named Desire* (1947), won a Pulitzer Prize. It is a study of the mental and moral ruin of Blanche DuBois, another former Southern belle, whose genteel pretensions are no match for the harsh realities symbolized by her brutish brother-in-law, Stanley Kowalski.

In 1953, *Camino Real*, a complex work set in a mythical, microcosmic town whose inhabitants include Lord Byron and Don Quixote, was a commercial failure, but his *Cat on a Hot Tin Roof* (1955), which exposes the emotional lies governing relationships in the family of a wealthy Southern planter, was awarded a Pulitzer Prize and was successfully filmed, as was *The Night of the Iguana* (1961), the story of a defrocked minister turned sleazy tour guide who finds God in a cheap Mexican hotel. *Suddenly Last Summer* (1958) deals with lobotomy, pederasty, and cannibalism, and in *Sweet Bird of Youth* (1959) the gigolo hero is castrated for having infected a Southern politician's daughter with venereal disease.

Williams was in ill health frequently during the 1960s, compounded by years of addiction to sleeping pills and liquor, problems that he struggled to overcome after a severe mental and physical breakdown in 1969. His later plays were unsuccessful, closing soon to poor reviews. They include *Vieux Carré* (1977), about down-and-outs in New Orleans; *A Lovely Sunday for Crève Coeur* (1978–79), about a fading belle in St. Louis during the Great Depression; and *Clothes for a Summer Hotel* (1980), centering on Zelda

Fitzgerald, wife of novelist F. Scott Fitzgerald, and on the people they knew.

Williams also wrote two novels, *The Roman Spring of Mrs. Stone* (1950) and *Moise and the World of Reason* (1975), essays, poetry, film scripts, short stories, and an autobiography, *Memoirs* (1975). His works won four Drama Critics' awards and were widely translated and performed around the world.

EDWARD ALBEE
(b. March 12, 1928, Washington, D.C.)

The dramatist and theatrical producer Edward Albee is best known for his play *Who's Afraid of Virginia Woolf?* (1962), which displays slashing insight and witty dialogue in its gruesome portrayal of married life.

Albee was the adopted child of a father who had for a time been the assistant general manager of a chain of vaudeville theatres then partially owned by the Albee family. At the time of Albee's adoption, however, both his parents were involved with owning and showing saddle horses. He had a difficult relationship with his parents, particularly with his mother, whom he saw as distant and unloving. Albee grew up in New York City and nearby Westchester county. He was educated at Choate School (graduated 1946) and at Trinity College in Hartford, Conn. (1946–47). He wrote poetry and an unpublished novel but turned to plays in the late 1950s.

Among Albee's early one-act plays, *The Zoo Story* (1959), *The Sandbox* (1959), and *The American Dream* (1961) were the most successful and established him as an astute critic of American values. But it is his first full-length play, *Who's Afraid of Virginia Woolf?* (film 1966), that remains his most important work. In this play a middle-aged professor, his wife, and a younger couple engage one night in an unrestrained drinking bout that is filled with malicious games, insults, humiliations, betrayals, savage witticisms, and painful, self-revealing confrontations. *Virginia Woolf* won immediate acclaim and established Albee as a major American playwright.

It was followed by a number of full-length works—including *A Delicate Balance* (1966; winner of a Pulitzer Prize), which was based in part on his mother's witty alcoholic sister, and *Three Tall Women* (1994; Pulitzer Prize). The latter play deals with Albee's perceptions and feelings about his mother and is a remarkable portrait achieved by presenting the interaction of three women, who resemble each other, at different stages of life. Among his other plays are *Tiny Alice* (1965), which begins as a philosophical discussion between a lawyer and a cardinal; *Seascape* (1975; also winner of a Pulitzer Prize), a poetic exploration of evolution; and *The Play About the Baby* (1998), on the mysteries of birth and parenthood.

Albee continued to dissect American morality in plays such as *The Goat; or, Who Is Sylvia?* (2002), which depicts the disintegration of a marriage in the wake of the revelation that the husband has engaged in bestiality. In *Occupant* (2001), Albee imagines the sculptor Louise Nevelson being interviewed after her death. Albee also expanded *The Zoo Story* into a two-act play, called *Peter and Jerry* (2004). The absurdist *Me, Myself, & I* (2007) trenchantly analyzes the relationship between a mother and her twin sons.

In addition to writing, Albee produced a number of plays and lectured at schools throughout the country. He was awarded the National Medal of Arts in 1996. A compilation of his essays and personal anecdotes, *Stretching My Mind*, was published in 2005. That year Albee also received a Tony Award for lifetime achievement.

Off-Broadway

In the theatre of the United States, the term "Off-Broadway" refers to small professional productions that have served since the mid-20th century as New York City's alternative to the commercially oriented theatres of Broadway.

Off-Broadway plays, usually produced on low budgets in small theatres, have tended to be freer in style and more imaginative than those on Broadway, where high production costs often oblige producers to rely on commercially safe attractions to the neglect of the more serious or experimental drama. The lower costs are permitted in part by more lenient union regulations governing minimum wages and number of personnel. The designations Broadway and Off-Broadway refer not so much to the location of the theatre as to its size and the scale of production. Most Broadway theatres are not located on Broadway itself but on the side streets adjacent to it. Some Off-Broadway theatres also are within the Broadway theatre district, but most are remote from midtown Manhattan. Off-Broadway theatres enjoyed a surge of growth in quality and importance after 1952, with the success of the director José Quintero's productions at the Circle in the Square theatre in Greenwich Village. In two decades of remarkable vitality, Off-Broadway introduced many important theatrical talents, such as the director Joseph Papp, whose later productions included free performances of Shakespeare in Central Park and who formed the Public Theatre, a multitheatre complex dedicated to experimental works. The works of such prizewinning American playwrights as Edward Albee, Charles Gordone, Paul Zindel, Sam Shepard, Lanford Wilson, and John Guare were first produced Off Broadway, along with the unconventional works of European avant-garde dramatists such as Eugène Ionesco, Ugo Betti, Jean Genet, Samuel Beckett, and Harold Pinter and revivals of Bertolt Brecht and Eugene O'Neill. The small theatres also trained many noted performers and experts in lighting, costume, and set design.

Like Broadway, Off-Broadway theatres began to suffer from soaring costs, which stimulated the emergence in the early 1960s of still less expensive and more daring productions, quickly labeled Off-Off-Broadway. The most successful of these have included such groups as The Negro Ensemble Company, La MaMa Experimental Theatre Club, the Open Theatre, Manhattan Theatre Club, Ensemble Studio Theatre, and Roundabout.

THE OFF-BROADWAY ASCENDANCY

The centre of American drama shifted from Broadway to Off-Broadway and Off-Off-Broadway with works such as Jack Gelber's *The Connection* (1959). American playwrights, collaborating with the Living Theatre, the Open Theatre, and other adventurous new companies, were increasingly free to write radical and innovative plays. David Rabe's *The Basic Training of Pavlo Hummel* (1971) and *Sticks and Bones* (1972) satirized America's militaristic nationalism and cultural shallowness. David Mamet won a New York Drama Critics' Circle Award for *American Buffalo* (1976). In plays such as *Glengarry Glen Ross* (1984), he brilliantly showed how men reveal their hopes and frustrations obliquely, through their language, and in *Oleanna* (1992) he fired a major salvo in the gender wars over sexual harassment.

Amiri Baraka (LeRoi Jones) and Ed Bullins inspired an angry black nationalist theatre. Baraka's *Dutchman* and *The Slave* (1964) effectively dramatized racial confrontation, while Bullins's *In the Wine Time* (1968) made use of "street" lyricism. Maria Irene Fornes's *Fefu and Her Friends* (1977) proved remarkable in its exploration of women's relationships. A clear indication of Off-Broadway's ascendancy in American drama came in 1979 when Sam Shepard, a prolific and experimental playwright, won the Pulitzer Prize for *Buried Child*. Shepard's earlier work, such as *The*

Off-Off Broadway and Regional Theatre

During the 1960s, a strong avant-garde theatre movement known as Off-Off Broadway emerged in New York City. The name is a play on the term "Off-Broadway" as well as a geographic description: Most such venues tend to be far removed from Broadway theatres—indeed, some have argued that all American regional theatres should be considered Off-Off Broadway. The Caffe Cino, which opened in 1958, was the earliest Off-Off Broadway locale, providing an experimental milieu that welcomed Beat poetry, music, and "happenings." The Living Theatre, among Off-Off Broadway's most overtly political repertory companies, was founded by Julian Beck and Judith Malina in 1947 to explore new and classic works in unorthodox locales with explicitly agitational intent. Café La Mama (later renamed La MaMa Experimental Theatre Club) was started in 1961 by Ellen Stewart and served as home to numerous companies.

Among other early influential groups were Joseph Chaikin's Open Theatre, Richard Schechner's Performance Group, the Negro Ensemble Company, Mabou Mines, Richard Foreman's Ontological-Hysteric Theater, the Wooster Group, and Joseph Papp's New York Shakespeare Festival (where *Hair* premiered in 1967 and the Broadway mainstay *A Chorus Line* had its start in 1975). Many groups explored ritual, sexuality, primitivism, and political conflict in productions that sought to challenge the barriers between actor and audience. At its best the Off-Off Broadway movement generated great excitement and vitality, but at its worst its works displayed gratuitous violence and self-indulgence and alienated the audience it set out to engage.

As Broadway and Off-Broadway became increasingly commercialized, various American regional companies offered more innovative works. Most companies were not defined by a "house style" of performance or repertoire. They tended to offer an eclectic mix of traditional classics and modern experimental plays, and they often produced world premieres by noted writers. Leading companies during the second half of the 20th century included the American Repertory Theatre of

Cambridge, Mass.; the Long Wharf Theatre and the Yale Repertory Theatre, both of New Haven, Conn.; the Goodman Theatre and the Steppenwolf Theatre, both of Chicago; the Guthrie Theater of Minneapolis, Minn.; the Alley Theatre of Houston; the Actors Theatre of Louisville, Ky.; the American Conservatory Theater and the Berkeley Repertory Theatre of San Francisco; and the La Jolla Playhouse of San Diego. Their continued existence at the turn of the 21st century as subscription houses offering seasons of plays confirmed the vitality of American theatre despite the inroads made on audiences' attention by film, television, and other popular media.

Tooth of Crime (1972), was rooted both in the rock scene and counterculture of the 1960s and in the mythic world of the American West. He reached his peak with a series of offbeat dramas dealing with fierce family conflict, including *Curse of the Starving Class* (1976), *True West* (1980), *Fool for Love* (1983), and *A Lie of the Mind* (1986).

Other important new voices in American drama were the prolific Lanford Wilson, Pulitzer winner for *Talley's Folly* (1979); John Guare, who created serious farce in *The House of Blue Leaves* (1971) and fresh social drama in *Six Degrees of Separation* (1990); and Ntozake Shange, whose "choreopoem" *For Colored Girls Who Have Considered Suicide/When the Rainbow Is Enuf* moved to Broadway in 1976. Other well-received women playwrights included Marsha Norman, Beth Henley, Tina Howe, and Wendy Wasserstein. In a series of plays that included *Ma Rainey's Black Bottom* (1984), *Fences* (1987), for which he won a Pulitzer Prize, and *Joe Turner's Come and Gone* (1986), August Wilson emerged as the most powerful black playwright of the 1980s. Devoting each play to a different decade of life in the 20th century, he won a second Pulitzer Prize, for *The Piano Lesson* (1990), and completed the 10-play cycle in 2005, shortly before his death.

The Living Theatre

The Living Theatre is a theatrical repertory company that was founded in New York City in 1947 by Julian Beck and Judith Malina. It is known for its innovative production of experimental drama, often on radical themes, and for its confrontations with tradition, authority, and sometimes audiences.

The group struggled during the 1950s, producing little-known, new, and experimental plays by such writers as Gertrude Stein, Luigi Pirandello, Alfred Jarry, T.S. Eliot, and others. Its first big success came with its 1959 production of *The Connection*, Jack Gelber's drama of drug addiction. In 1961 the company made a successful tour of Europe with *The Connection* and with plays by Bertolt Brecht and William Carlos Williams.

On returning to New York City, the political views of the members of the troupe—nonviolent protest and anarchism—came to the fore in their work. In 1963 they produced Kenneth H. Brown's *The Brig*, a play that depicted military discipline as dehumanizing. The U.S. Internal Revenue Service demanded payment of a large sum in admissions taxes that the constantly impoverished group had collected and had used to pay production costs while vainly seeking tax-exempt status. Beck and Malina were tried and convicted of tax law violation and jailed briefly, and the Living Theatre was closed.

In 1964 the company took up "voluntary exile" in Europe. Now influenced by Oriental mysticism, gestalt therapy techniques, and an Artaudian desire to abolish the distinction between art and life, the Living Theatre moved toward deliberately shocking and confronting its audiences in such works as *Paradise Now* (1968), in which the actors performed rituals, provoked arguments, and carried on until members of the audience left. A collaborative play cycle entitled *The Legacy of Cain* was the focus of the Living Theatre's performances in the 1970s. For this work, they shunned the usual theatrical venues, instead performing for free in public spaces and in such unusual places as the site of a Pittsburgh steel mill, a Brazilian prison, and the streets of Palermo, Italy. The company took up the theatre venue

again in the 1980s, while continuing to emphasize the unusual
and innovative in its performances, including *The Body of God*, a
collective collaboration with homeless people. Cofounder Beck
died in 1985 and was replaced as codirector by Hanon Reznikov,
a longtime veteran of the troupe. After 1999 the company
divided its time between New York City and its European head-
quarters near Genoa, Italy.

The anguish of the AIDS epidemic proved a dark
inspiration to many gay playwrights, especially Tony
Kushner, who had gained attention with *A Bright Room
Called Day* (1991), set in Germany in 1932–33; he won
Broadway fame with his epically ambitious two-part
drama *Angels in America* (1991–92), which combined comedy with pain, symbolism with personal history, and
invented characters with historical ones. A committed
political writer, Kushner often focused on public themes.
His later plays included *Slavs!* (1996) and the timely
Homebody/Kabul (2001), a brilliant monologue followed by
a drama set in Taliban-controlled Afghanistan. After writing several Off-Broadway plays about Chinese Americans,
David Henry Hwang achieved critical and commercial
success on Broadway with his gender-bending drama *M.
Butterfly* (1988). Richard Nelson found an enthusiastic following in London for literate plays such as *Some Americans
Abroad* (1989) and *Two Shakespearean Actors* (1990), while
Richard Greenberg depicted Jewish American life and
both gay and straight relationships in *Eastern Standard*
(1989), *The American Plan* (1990), and *Take Me Out* (2002),
the last about a gay baseball player who reveals his homosexuality to his teammates. Donald Margulies dealt more
directly with Jewish family life in *The Loman Family Picnic*
(1989). He also explored the ambitions and relationships

of artists in such plays as *Sight Unseen* (1992) and *Collected Stories* (1998).

The 1990s also saw the emergence of several talented women playwrights. Paula Vogel repeatedly focused on hot-button moral issues with humour and compassion, dealing with prostitution in *The Oldest Profession* (1981), AIDS in *The Baltimore Waltz* (1992), pornography in *Hot 'n' Throbbing* (1994), and the sexual abuse of minors in *How I Learned to Drive* (1997). A young African American playwright, Suzan-Lori Parks, gained increasing recognition with her surreal pageant *The America Play* (1993), a ghetto adaptation of *The Scarlet Letter* called *In the Blood* (1999), and *Topdog/Underdog* (2001), a partly symbolic tale of conflict between two brothers (named Lincoln and Booth) that reminded critics of Sam Shepard's fratricidal *True West*. Other well-received works included Heather McDonald's *An Almost Holy Picture* (1995), a one-man play about the spiritual life of a preacher; poet Naomi Wallace's *One Flea Spare* (1995), set in London during the Great Plague of 1665; and Margaret Edson's *Wit* (1995), about the slow, poignant cancer death of a literary scholar whose life has been shaped by the eloquence and wit of Metaphysical poetry. Feminism helped free these writers to develop a rich range of subjects rarely seen on the American stage.

NOTABLE DRAMATISTS OF THE AGE, IN DEPTH

The growth of the Off-Broadway and Off-Off-Broadway movements led to increased opportunities for a wide variety of dramatists to make a name for themselves in the years since World War II. As touched upon in the preceeding section, all of the following playwrights got their starts far from the glitz of Broadway, but nevertheless they became some of the leading American dramatists of the past half-century.

AMIRI BARAKA
(b. October 7, 1934, Newark, N.J.)

Born Everett LeRoi Jones, Amiri Baraka presents the experiences and anger of black Americans with an affirmation of black life.

Jones graduated from Howard University (B.A., 1953) and served in the U.S. Air Force. After military duty, he joined the Beat movement, attended graduate school, and in 1961 published his first major collection of poetry, *Preface to a Twenty Volume Suicide Note*. In 1964 his play *Dutchman* appeared Off-Broadway to critical acclaim. In its depiction of an encounter between a white woman and a black intellectual, it exposes the suppressed anger and hostility of American blacks toward the dominant white culture. After the assassination of Malcolm X, Jones took the name Amiri Baraka and began to espouse black nationalism.

In 1965 he founded the Black Arts Repertory Theatre in Harlem. He published much during this period, including *Black Art* (1966) and *Black Magic* (1969). In addition to poetry and drama, Baraka wrote several collections of essays, an autobiographical novel titled *The System of Dante's Hell* (1965), and short stories. In the mid-1970s he became a Marxist, although his goals remained similar. "I [still] see art as a weapon and a weapon of revolution," he said. "It's just now that I define revolution in Marxist terms." In addition to writing, Baraka taught at several American universities. *The Autobiography of LeRoi Jones/ Amiri Baraka* was published in 1984.

JACK GELBER
(b. April 12, 1932, Chicago, Ill.—d. May 9, 2003, New York, N.Y.)

Playwright Jack Gelber was known for his play *The Connection* (performed 1959; published 1960), and for his association with the Living Theatre, an innovative, experimental theatre group.

After graduating from the University of Illinois in Urbana, Gelber began working with the struggling Living Theatre group in New York City. His first play, *The Connection*, is historically important for its disintegration of the traditional relationship between audience and actor. It was a breakthrough for the Living Theatre, and both the production and the playwright received wide notice.

Set in a slum apartment, the play was staged to suggest a naturalistic scene, with actors already on stage as the audience arrived (as if the audience were seeing life, not a play, in progress). This nontraditional technique was supported by other unconventional techniques: presenting an actor as an audience member, using the theatre aisles as a performance area, and having the actors (who represented drug addicts) panhandle the audience during the play's intermission. The play was imaginatively and brilliantly produced by the Living Theatre, although for all its appearance of improvisation, it was tightly structured. *The Connection* won an Obie Award (presented by the *Village Voice* newspaper) for best new play, and a film version appeared in 1962.

The Apple (1961), Gelber's second play, also was written expressly for the Living Theatre. Plotted around the growing madness of an actor during a play rehearsal, its second act was written from the mad actor's point of view, thus also breaking with the conventions of theatre. Less successful than its predecessor, *The Apple* had a run of 69 performances. With the departure of the Living Theatre for Europe, however, Gelber lost a performance group ideally suited to his drama.

Gelber's *Square in the Eye* (1965), a multimedia theatre piece, and the rest of his later plays—including *The Cuban Thing* (1968), *Sleep* (1972), and *Rehearsal* (1976)—continued to challenge theatrical conventions, but none matched the popular or critical success of his first play. In addition to writing plays, Gelber taught drama at several American colleges and universities and wrote the novel *On Ice* (1964).

JOHN GUARE
(b. Feb. 5, 1938, New York, N.Y.)

John Guare is known for his innovative and often absurdist dramas.

Guare, who at age 11 produced his first play for friends and family, was educated at Georgetown University, Washington, D.C. (B.A., 1960), and at Yale University (M.F.A., 1963). He then began staging short plays, primarily in New York City, where he helped to found the Eugene O'Neill Memorial Theatre Playwrights' Conference. His first notable works—*Muzeeka* (1968), about American soldiers of the Vietnam War who have television contracts, and *Cop-Out* (1968)—satirize the American media.

In 1971 Guare earned critical acclaim for *The House of Blue Leaves* (filmed for television, 1987), a farce about a zookeeper who murders his insane wife after he fails as a songwriter. *Two Gentlemen of Verona* (1972; with Mel Shapiro), a rock-musical modernization of William Shakespeare's comedy, won the Tony and New York Drama Critics Circle awards for best musical of 1971–72. Guare dealt with such issues as success in *Marco Polo Sings a Solo* (1977) and *Rich and Famous* (1977) and parent–child relationships in *Landscape of the Body* (1978) and *Bosoms and*

Neglect (1980). The plays *Lydie Breeze* (1982), *Gardenia* (1982), and *Women and Water* (1990) make up a family saga set in Nantucket, Mass., in the second half of the 19th century.

Other works include *Four Baboons Adoring the Sun, and Other Plays* (1993) and *The War Against the Kitchen Sink* (1996). His one-act play *The General of Hot Desire*, first performed in 1998, is an unsympathetic adaptation of the Bible that takes as one of its starting points Shakespeare's sonnet number 154, from which the title of the play is taken. *Lake Hollywood* (2000) chronicles the lives of dissatisfied people and the futility of their idolization of celebrities, and *Chaucer in Rome* (2002), a sequel to *The House of Blue Leaves*, satirizes art, religion, and fame. *A Few Stout Individuals* (2003) is a colourful account of the memories and delusions of a dying Ulysses S. Grant. Guare also wrote several screenplays, including the 1993 adaptation of his play *Six Degrees of Separation*.

TONY KUSHNER
(b. July 16, 1956, New York, N.Y.)

The dramatist Tony Kushner became one of the most highly acclaimed playwrights of his generation after the debut of his two-part play *Angels in America* (1990, 1991).

Kushner grew up in Lake Charles, La., and attended Columbia University and New York University. His early plays include *La Fin de la Baleine: An Opera for the Apocalypse* (1983), *A Bright Room Called Day* (1985), *Yes, Yes, No, No* (1985), and *Stella* (1987). His major work, *Angels in America: A Gay Fantasia on National Themes*, consists of two lengthy plays that deal with political issues and the AIDS epidemic in the 1980s while meditating on change and loss—two prominent themes throughout Kushner's oeuvre. The first part, *Millennium Approaches* (1990), won a Pulitzer

Tony Kushner is best known for his avant-garde two-part play, Angels in America, *which addresses themes of alienation and loss in the face of the 1980s AIDS epidemic.* Kevin Winter/Getty Images

Prize and a Tony Award for best play; the second, *Perestroika* (1991), also won a Tony Award for best play. *Angels in America* proved to be extremely popular for a work of its imposing length (the two parts run seven hours in total), and it was adapted for an Emmy Award-winning television film in 2003.

Later plays include *Slavs!* (1994); *A Dybbuk; or, Between Two Worlds* (1995), an adaptation of S. Ansky's Yiddish classic *Der Dibek*; *Henry Box Brown; or, The Mirror of Slavery* (1998); and *Homebody/Kabul* (1999), which addresses the relationship between Afghanistan and the West. Kushner also wrote the book for the musical *Caroline, or Change* (1999). His unfinished *Only We Who Guard the Mystery Shall Be Unhappy*, written in response to the Iraq War, was performed in a number of readings in 2004. His translation of Bertolt Brecht's *Mother Courage and Her Children* was staged in New York City in 2006. Kushner's *The Intelligent Homosexual's Guide to Capitalism and Socialism with a Key to the Scriptures* (2009) is a naturalistic drama about an extended family of intellectuals dealing with their patriarch's desire to commit suicide.

In addition to his work for the stage, he cowrote (with Eric Roth) the screenplay for Stephen Spielberg's film *Munich* (2005). Kushner also authored the children's book *Brundibar* (2003; illustrated by Maurice Sendak) and coedited (with Alisa Solomon) the essay collection *Wrestling with Zion: Progressive Jewish-American Responses to the Israeli-Palestinian Conflict* (2003).

DAVID MAMET

(b. Nov. 30, 1947, Chicago, Ill.)

The American playwright, director, and screenwriter David Mamet is noted for his often desperate working-class characters and for his distinctive, colloquial, and frequently profane dialogue.

Mamet began writing plays while attending Goddard College, Plainfield, Vt. (B.A., 1969). Returning to Chicago, where many of his plays were first staged, he worked at various factory jobs, at a real estate agency, and as a taxi driver. All these experiences provided background for his plays. In 1973 he cofounded a theatre company in Chicago. He also taught drama at several American colleges and universities.

Mamet's early plays include *Duck Variations* (produced 1972), in which two elderly Jewish men sit on a park bench and trade misinformation on various subjects. In *Sexual Perversity in Chicago* (produced 1974; filmed as *About Last Night...* [1986]), a couple's budding sexual and emotional relationship is destroyed by their friends' interference. *American Buffalo* (1976; film 1996) concerns dishonest business practices; *A Life in the Theatre* (1977) explores the teacher–student relationship; and *Speed-the-Plow* (1987) is a black comedy about avaricious Hollywood scriptwriters.

Glengarry Glen Ross (1983; film 1992), a drama of desperate real estate salesmen, won the 1984 Pulitzer Prize for drama. *Oleanna* (1992; film 1994) probes the definition of sexual harassment through the interactions between a professor and his female student. Mamet attempted to address the accusations of chauvinism frequently directed at his work with *Boston Marriage* (1999), a drawing-room comedy about two lesbians. *Dr. Faustus* (2004) puts a contemporary spin on the German Faust legend, and *Romance* (2005) comically skewers the prejudices of a Jewish man and his Protestant lawyer. *November* (2008) is a farcical portrait of a U.S. president running for reelection. In all these works, Mamet used the rhythms and rhetoric of everyday speech to delineate character, describe intricate relationships, and drive dramatic development.

Mamet wrote screenplays for a number of motion pictures, including *The Postman Always Rings Twice* (1981); *The Verdict* (1982), for which he received an Academy Award nomination; *Rising Sun* (1993); *Wag the Dog* (1997), for which he received another Academy Award nomination; and *Hannibal* (2001), all adaptations of novels. He both wrote and directed the motion pictures *House of Games* (1987), *Homicide* (1991), and *The Spanish Prisoner* (1998). In 1999 he directed *The Winslow Boy*, which he had adapted from a play by Terence Rattigan. *State and Main* (2000), a well-received ensemble piece written and directed by Mamet, depicts the trials and tribulations of a film crew shooting in a small town. He also applied his dual talents to *Heist* (2001), a crime thriller, and *Redbelt* (2008), a latter-day samurai film about the misadventures of a martial arts instructor. Mamet created and wrote *The Unit*, a television drama that premiered in 2006, which centred on the activities of a secret U.S. Army unit.

Mamet also wrote fiction, including *The Village* (1994); *The Old Religion* (1997), a novelization of an actual anti-Semitic lynching in the American South; and *Wilson: A Consideration of the Sources* (2000), which speculates on the havoc that might be caused by a crash of the Internet. He published several volumes articulating his stance on various aspects of theatre and film, including *On Directing Film* (1992), *Three Uses of the Knife* (1996), and *True and False: Heresy and Common Sense for the Actor* (1999). Compilations of his essays and experiences include *Writing in Restaurants* (1987), *Make-Believe Town* (1996), and *Bambi vs. Godzilla: On the Nature, Purpose, and Practice of the Movie Business* (2007). Mamet addressed the topic of anti-Semitism in *The Wicked Son: Anti-Semitism, Self-Hatred, and the Jews* (2006). He wrote several plays for children as well.

SUZAN-LORI PARKS
(b. 1964, Fort Knox, Ky.)

In 2002 playwright Suzan-Lori Parks became the first black woman playwright to win a Pulitzer Prize, for *Topdog/Underdog* (2001).

Parks, who was writing stories at age five, had a peri-patetic childhood as the daughter of a military officer. She attended Mount Holyoke College, South Hadley, Mass. (B.A. [cum laude], 1985), where James Baldwin, who taught a writing class there, encouraged her to try playwriting. She wrote her first play, *The Sinner's Place* (produced 1984), while still in school. She won Obie Awards for her third play, *Imperceptible Mutabilities in the Third Kingdom* (produced 1989), and for her eighth, *Venus* (produced 1996), about a South African Khoisan woman taken to England as a sideshow attraction.

Parks's other plays include *The Death of the Last Black Man in the Whole Entire World* (produced 1990); *The America Play* (produced 1994), about a man obsessed with Abraham Lincoln; and *In the Blood* (produced 1999), which updates Nathaniel Hawthorne's *The Scarlet Letter*. In 2006–07 she oversaw a project that coordinated performances across the United States of the plays she had written, one per day over the course of a year, in 2002–03 (collected as *365 Days/365 Plays* [2006]). Parks also wrote radio plays (*Pickling* [1990]), screenplays (*Girl 6* [1996]), and teleplays (*Their Eyes Were Watching God* [2005], an adaptation of Zora Neale Hurston's novel). Parks's first novel, *Getting*

Mother's Body, was published in 2003. Her writing has been praised for its wild poetry, its irreverence, its humour, and its concurrent profundity. She received a MacArthur Foundation fellowship in 2001.

NTOZAKE SHANGE
(b. Oct. 18, 1948, Trenton, N.J.)

An American author of plays, poetry, and fiction, Ntozake Shange is noted for the strong feminist themes and racial and sexual anger of her writings.

Born Paulette Williams, she attended Barnard College (B.A., 1970) and the University of Southern California (M.A., 1973). In 1971 she changed her name to Ntozake Shange, which she took from the language of the Xhosa tribe of South Africa. From 1972 to 1975 she taught humanities, women's studies, and Afro-American studies at California colleges. During this period she also made public appearances as a dancer and reciter of poetry. Her 1975 theatre piece *For Colored Girls Who Have Considered Suicide/When the Rainbow Is Enuf* quickly brought her fame. Written for seven actors, *For Colored Girls* is a group of 20 poems on the power of black women to survive in the face of despair and pain. It ran for seven months Off-Broadway in New York City, then moved to Broadway and was subsequently produced throughout the United States and broadcast on television.

Shange created a number of other theatre works that employed poetry, dance, and music (known as "choreo-poems") while abandoning conventions of plot and character development. One of the most popular of these was her 1980 adaptation of Bertolt Brecht's *Mother Courage,* featuring a black family in the time of the American Civil War. Some of Shange's other works for the stage are *Where the Mississippi Meets the Amazon* (1977), *Three Views of Mt. Fuji* (1987), and *The Love Space Demands: A Continuing Saga* (1992).

Shange's poetry collections include *Nappy Edges* (1978) and *Ridin' the Moon in Texas* (1987). She also published the novels *Sassafrass, Cypress & Indigo* (1982), about the diverging lives of three sisters and their mother; the semiautobiographical *Betsey Brown* (1985); and *Liliane: Resurrection of the Daughter* (1994), a coming-of-age story about a wealthy black woman in the American South. In addition, Shange wrote a number of children's books, including *Whitewash* (1997), *Daddy Says* (2003), and *Ellington Was Not a Street* (2004).

SAM SHEPARD
(b. Nov. 5, 1943, Fort Sheridan [near Highland Park], Ill.)

Playwright and actor Sam Shepard is best known for his plays that adroitly blend images of the American West, Pop motifs, science fiction, and other elements of popular and youth culture.

As the son of a career army father, Shepard spent his childhood on military bases across the United States and in Guam before his family settled on a farm in Duarte, Calif. After a year of agricultural studies in college, he joined a touring company of actors and, in 1963, moved to New York City to pursue his theatrical interests. His earliest attempts at playwriting, a rapid succession of one-act plays, found a receptive audience in Off-Off-Broadway productions. In the 1965–66 season Shepard won Obie Awards for his plays *Chicago, Icarus's Mother,* and *Red Cross.*

Shepard lived in England from 1971 to 1974, and two notable plays of this period—*The Tooth of Crime* (1972) and

183

Geography of a Horse Dreamer (1974)—premiered in London. In late 1974 he became playwright-in-residence at the Magic Theatre in San Francisco, where most of his subsequent plays were first produced.

Shepard's works of the mid-1970s showed a heightening of earlier techniques and themes. In *Killer's Head* (1975), for example, the rambling monologue, a Shepard stock-in-trade, blends horror and banality in a murderer's last thoughts before electrocution. *Angel City* (1976) depicts the destructive machinery of the Hollywood entertainment industry. Finally, *Suicide in B-Flat* (1976) exploits the potential of music as an expression of character.

Beginning in the late 1970s, Shepard applied his unconventional dramatic vision to a more conventional dramatic form, the family tragedy. *Curse of the Starving Class* (1976), the Pulitzer Prize–winning *Buried Child* (1978), and *True West* (1980) are linked thematically in their examination of troubled and tempestuous blood relationships in a fragmented society.

Shepard also returned to acting in the late 1970s, winning critical accolades for his performances in such films as *Days of Heaven* (1978), *Resurrection* (1980), *The Right Stuff* (1983), and *Fool for Love* (1985), which was written by Shepard and based on his 1983 play of the same name. He also appeared in *The Pelican Brief* (1993), *Snow Falling on Cedars* (1999), *All the Pretty Horses* (2000), which was based on a novel by Cormac McCarthy, *Black Hawk Down* (2001), *The Notebook* (2004), and *The Assassination of Jesse James by the Coward Robert Ford* (2007).

His other plays include *La Turista* (1966), *Operation Sidewinder* (1970), *The Unseen Hand* (1970), *Seduced* (1979), *A Lie of the Mind* (1986), *Simpatico* (1994), *The God of Hell* (2004), and *Ages of the Moon* (2009). In 1986 Shepard was elected to the American Academy of Arts and Letters.

Wendy Wasserstein's plays often feature women coming of age toward the end of the 20th century. There is a particular focus on those trying to succeed in male-dominated areas. Scott Gries/Getty Images

WENDY WASSERSTEIN

(b. Oct. 18, 1950, Brooklyn, N.Y.—d. Jan. 30, 2006, New York, N.Y.)

Wendy Wasserstein was a playwright whose work probes, with humour and sensibility, the predicament facing educated women who came of age in the second half of the 20th century. Her drama *The Heidi Chronicles* (1988) was awarded both a Pulitzer Prize and a Tony Award in 1989.

Wasserstein was educated at Mount Holyoke College (B.A., 1971) and City College of the City University of New York (M.A., 1973), where she studied creative writing with playwright Israel Horovitz and novelist Joseph Heller. In 1976 she received an M.F.A. from Yale University.

Wasserstein's first play, *Any Woman Can't* (1973), is a cutting farce on one of her major themes—a woman's attempts to succeed in an environment traditionally dominated by men. Two other early works are *Uncommon Women and Others* (1975; revised and expanded, 1977) and *Isn't It Romantic* (1981), which explore women's attitudes toward marriage and society's expectations of women. In *The Heidi Chronicles*, a successful art historian discovers that her independent life choices have alienated her from men as well as women. *The Sisters Rosensweig* (1992) continues the theme into middle age. Later plays include *An American Daughter* (1997) and *Third* (2005).

Wasserstein's other works include an adaptation for television of the John Cheever short story *The Sorrows of Gin* (1979); the play *When Dinah Shore Ruled the Earth* (1975; with Christopher Durang); *The Man in a Case* (1986), an adaptation of Anton Chekhov's short story; a musical, *Miami* (1986); and a children's book, *Pamela's First Musical* (1996). She also wrote several collections of essays, including *Shiksa Goddess* (2001).

AUGUST WILSON
(b. April 27, 1945, Pittsburgh, Penn.—d. Oct. 2, 2005, Seattle, Wash.)

August Wilson was a playwright, author of a cycle of plays, each set in a different decade of the 20th century, about black American life. He won Pulitzer Prizes for *Fences* (1986) and for *The Piano Lesson* (1990).

Named for his father, a white German immigrant who was largely absent from the family, Frederick August Kittel later adopted his mother's last name. Wilson's early years were spent in the Hill District of Pittsburgh, a poor but lively neighbourhood that became the setting for most of his plays. Primarily self-educated, he quit school at age

15 after being accused of plagiarizing a paper. He later joined the black aesthetic movement in the late 1960s, became the cofounder and director of Black Horizons Theatre in Pittsburgh (1968), and published poetry in such journals as *Black World* (1971) and *Black Lines* (1972).

In 1978 Wilson moved to St. Paul, Minn., and in the early 1980s he wrote several plays, including *Jitney* (2000; first produced 1982). Focused on cab drivers in the 1970s, it underwent subsequent revisions as part of his historical cycle. His first major play, *Ma Rainey's Black Bottom*, opened on Broadway in 1984 and was a critical and financial success. Set in Chicago in 1927, the play centres on a verbally abusive blues singer, her fellow black musicians, and their white manager. *Fences*, first produced in 1985, is about a conflict between a father and son in the 1950s; it received a Tony Award for best play. Wilson's chronicle of the black American experience continued with *Joe Turner's Come and Gone* (1988), a play about the lives of residents of a boardinghouse in 1911; *The Piano Lesson*, set in the 1930s and concerning a family's ambivalence about selling an heirloom; and *Two Trains Running* (1992), whose action takes place in a coffeehouse in the 1960s. *Seven Guitars* (1996), the seventh play of the cycle, is set among a group of friends who reunite in 1948 following the death of a local blues guitarist.

Subsequent plays in the series are *King Hedley II* (2005; first produced 1999), an account of an ex-con's efforts to rebuild his life in the 1980s, and *Gem of the Ocean* (first produced 2003), which takes place in 1904 and centres on Aunt Ester, a 287-year-old spiritual healer mentioned in previous plays, and a man who seeks her help. Wilson completed the cycle with *Radio Golf* (first produced 2005). Set in the 1990s, the play concerns the fate of Aunt Ester's house, which is slated to be torn down by real estate developers. Music, particularly jazz and blues, is a recurrent theme in Wilson's works, and its cadence is echoed in the lyrical, vernacular nature of his dialogue.

Wilson received numerous honours during his career, including seven New York Drama Critics' Circle Awards for best play. He also held Guggenheim and Rockefeller fellowships. Shortly after his death, the Virginia Theater on Broadway was renamed in his honour.

LANFORD WILSON
(b. April 13, 1937, Lebanon, Mo.)

Lanford Eugene Wilson is a pioneer of the Off-Off-Broadway and regional theatre movements. His plays are known for experimental staging, simultaneous dialogue, and deferred character exposition. He won a 1980 Pulitzer Prize for *Talley's Folly* (1979).

Wilson attended schools in Missouri, San Diego, California, and Chicago before moving to New York City in 1962. From 1963 his plays were produced regularly at Off-Off-Broadway theatres such as Caffe Cino and La MaMa Experimental Theatre Club *Home Free!* and *The Madness of Lady Bright* (published together in 1968) are two one-act plays first performed in 1964, the former involving a pair of incestuous siblings and the latter featuring an aging transvestite. *Balm in Gilead* (1965), Wilson's first full-length play, is set in a crowded world of hustlers and junkies. *The Rimers of Eldritch* (1967) examines life in a small town.

In 1969, along with longtime associate Marshall W. Mason and others, he founded the Circle Theatre (later Circle Repertory Company), a regional theatre in New York City. Wilson remained involved with Circle Repertory until 1996, when it closed. Wilson achieved commercial success with *The Great Nebula in Orion* (1971), *The Hot l Baltimore* (1973), and *The Mound Builders* (1975).

He also wrote a cycle of plays about the effects of war on a family from Missouri, including *The 5th of July* (1978; televised 1982), *Talley's Folly*, *A Tale Told* (1981), and *Talley and Son* (1985). His other plays include *The Gingham Dog* (1969), *Lemon Sky* (1970; televised 1987), *Burn This* (1987), and *Redwood Curtain* (1993; televised 1995), about a young adopted woman's search for information about the Vietnamese woman and American GI who are her real parents. The plays *Sympathetic Magic* (1998) and *Book of Days* (2000) received mixed critical reviews. Some of Wilson's plays are gathered in *Four Short Plays* (1994) and *Collected Plays, 1965–1970* (1996).

CHAPTER 5

LITERARY CRITICISM AND THEORY FROM 1945

Until his death in 1972, Edmund Wilson solidified his reputation as one of America's most versatile and distinguished men of letters. The novelist John Updike inherited Wilson's chair at the *New Yorker* and turned out an extraordinary flow of critical reviews collected in volumes such as *Hugging the Shore* (1983) and *Odd Jobs* (1991). Gore Vidal brought together his briskly readable essays of four decades—critical, personal, and political—in *United States* (1993). Susan Sontag's essays on difficult European writers, avant-garde film, politics, photography, and the language of illness embodied the probing intellectual spirit of the 1960s. In *A Second Flowering* (1973) and *The Dream of the Golden Mountains* (1980), Malcolm Cowley looked back at the writers between the world wars who had always engaged him. Alfred Kazin wrote literary history (*An American Procession* [1984], *God and the American Writer* [1997]) and autobiography (*Starting Out in the Thirties* [1965], *New York Jew* [1978]), while Irving Howe produced studies at the crossroads of literature and politics, such as *Politics and the Novel* (1957), as well as a major history of Jewish immigrants in New York, *World of Our Fathers* (1976).

The iconoclastic literary criticism of Leslie Fiedler, such as, for example, *Love and Death in the American Novel* (1960), was marked by its provocative application of Freudian ideas to American literature. In his later work he

Susan Sontag

(b. Jan. 16, 1933, New York, N.Y.—d. Dec. 28, 2004, New York)

In addition to essays on modern culture, Susan Sontag wrote screenplays and criticism, and edited selected writings of other authors. Markus Benk/AFP/Getty Images

The intellectual and writer Susan Sontag is best known for her essays on modern culture.

Sontag (who was born Susan Rosenblatt but later adopted her stepfather's name) was reared in Tucson, Ariz., and in Los Angeles. She attended the University of California, Berkeley, for one year and then transferred to the University of Chicago, from which she graduated in 1951. She studied English literature (M.A., 1954) and philosophy (M.A., 1955) at Harvard University and taught philosophy at several colleges and universities before the publication of her first novel, *The Benefactor* (1963). During the early 1960s she also wrote a number of essays and reviews, most of which were published in such periodicals as the *New York Review of Books, Commentary*, and *Partisan Review*. Some of these short pieces were collected in *Against Interpretation, and Other Essays* (1966). Her second novel, *Death Kit* (1967), was followed by another collection of essays, *Styles of Radical Will* (1969). Her later critical works included *On Photography* (1977), *Illness as Metaphor* (1978), *Under the Sign of Saturn* (1980), and *AIDS and Its Metaphors* (1989). She also wrote the historical novels *The Volcano Lover: A Romance* (1992) and *In America* (2000).

Sontag's essays are characterized by a serious philosophical approach to various aspects and personalities of modern culture.

She first came to national attention in 1964 with an essay entitled "Notes on 'Camp,'" in which she discussed the attributes of taste within the gay community. She also wrote on such subjects as theatre and film and such figures as writer Nathalie Sarraute, director Robert Bresson, and painter Francis Bacon. In addition to criticism and fiction, she wrote screenplays and edited selected writings of Roland Barthes and Antonin Artaud. Some of her later writings and speeches were collected in *At the Same Time: Essays and Speeches* (2007).

turned to popular culture as a source of revealing social and psychological patterns. A more subtle Freudian, Lionel Trilling, in *The Liberal Imagination* (1950) and other works, rejected Vernon L. Parrington's populist concept of literature as social reportage and insisted on the ability of literature to explore problematic human complexity. His criticism reflected the inward turn from politics toward "moral realism" that coincided with the Cold War. But the cultural and political conflicts of the 1960s revived the social approach among younger students of American literature, such as Henry Louis Gates, Jr., who emerged in the 1980s as a major critic, theorist, and editor of black writers in studies such as *Figures in Black* (1987) and *The Signifying Monkey* (1988). In the 1990s Gates evolved into a wide-ranging essayist, along with Cornel West, Stanley Crouch, bell hooks, Shelby Steele, Stephen Carter, Gerald Early, Michele Wallace, and other black social critics.

LITERARY BIOGRAPHY AND THE NEW JOURNALISM

The waning of the New Criticism, with its strict emphasis on the text, led not only to a surge of historical criticism and cultural theory but also to a flowering of literary biography. Major works included Leon Edel's five-volume study of Henry James (1953–72), Mark Schorer's *Sinclair Lewis: An American Life* (1961), Richard Ellmann's studies of James Joyce (1959) and Oscar Wilde (1988), R.W.B. Lewis's revealing biography of Edith Wharton (1975), Joseph Frank's five-volume biography of Dostoyevsky (1976–2002), Paul Zweig's brilliant study of Walt Whitman (1984), and Carol Brightman's exhaustive life of Mary McCarthy (1992).

One positive result of the accelerating complexity of post–World War II life was a body of distinguished journalism and social commentary. John Hersey's *Hiroshima* (1946) was a deliberately controlled, unemotional account of atomic holocaust. In *Notes of a Native Son* (1955), *Nobody Knows My Name* (1961), and *The Fire Next Time* (1963), the novelist James Baldwin published a body of the most eloquent essays written in the United States. Ralph Ellison's essays on race and culture in *Shadow and Act* (1964) and *Going to the Territory* (1986) were immensely influential. Norman Mailer's new journalism proved especially effective in capturing the drama of political conventions and large protest demonstrations. The novelist Joan Didion published two collections of incisive social and literary commentary, *Slouching Towards Bethlehem* (1968) and *The White Album* (1979). The title essay of the former collection was an honest investigation of the forces that gave colour and significance to the counterculture of the 1960s, a subject also explored with stylistic flourish by journalists as different as Tom Wolfe and Hunter S. Thompson. The surreal atmosphere of the Vietnam War, infused with rock music and drugs, gave impetus to subjective journalism such as Michael Herr's *Dispatches* (1977). The mood of the period also encouraged strong works of autobiography, such as Frank Conroy's *Stop-Time* (1967) and Lillian Hellman's personal and political memoirs, including *An Unfinished Woman* (1969) and *Scoundrel Time* (1976). Robert

AMERICAN LITERATURE FROM 1945 THROUGH TODAY

Hunter S. Thompson

(b. July 18, 1937, Louisville, Ky.—d. Feb. 20, 2005, Woody Creek, Colo.)

Journalist and author Hunter S. Thompson created the genre known as gonzo journalism, a highly personal style of reporting that made Thompson a counterculture icon.

Hunter Stockton Thompson, who had a number of run-ins with the law as a young man, joined the U.S. Air Force in 1956. He served as a sports editor for a base newspaper and continued his journalism career after being discharged in 1957. In 1965 he infiltrated the Hell's Angels motorcycle gang, an experience he recounted in *Hell's Angels* (1967). The book led to writing assignments for *Esquire*, *Harper's*, *Rolling Stone*, and other magazines. In addition to his irreverent political and cultural criticism, Thompson also began to attract attention for his larger-than-life persona, which was highlighted by drug- and alcohol-fueled adventures and a distaste for authority.

In 1970 Thompson introduced his subjective style of reporting with the article "The Kentucky Derby Is Decadent and Depraved," in which he was a central part of the story. A 1971 assignment for *Sports Illustrated* to cover a motorcycle race in Nevada resulted in perhaps his best-known work, *Fear and Loathing in Las Vegas: A Savage Journey to the Heart of the American Dream* (1972; film 1998), which became a contemporary classic and established the genre of gonzo journalism. First serialized in *Rolling Stone*, it documents the drug-addled road trip taken by Thompson (as his alter ego Raoul Duke) and his lawyer (Dr. Gonzo) while also discussing the end of the 1960s counterculture. The book featured frenetic artwork by Ralph Steadman, who illustrated many of Thompson's works. In *Fear and Loathing: On the Campaign Trail '72* (1973), Thompson chronicled the 1972 presidential campaigns of George McGovern and Richard Nixon. Later works include *The Great Shark Hunt* (1979), *Better Than Sex* (1994), and *Kingdom of Fear* (2003). Thompson died of a self-inflicted gunshot wound.

M. Pirsig's *Zen and the Art of Motorcycle Maintenance* (1974) defied all classification. Pirsig equated the emotional collapse of his central character with the disintegration of American workmanship and cultural values.

THEORY

The major New Critics and New York critics were followed by major but difficult academic critics, who preferred theory to close reading. European structuralism found little echo in the United States, but poststructuralist theorists such as Michel Foucault, Roland Barthes, and Jacques Derrida found a welcome in the less political atmosphere, marked by skepticism and defeat, that followed the 1960s. Four Yale professors joined Derrida to publish a group of essays, *Deconstruction and Criticism* (1979). Two of the contributors, Paul de Man and J. Hillis Miller, became leading exponents of deconstruction in the United States. The other two, Harold Bloom and Geoffrey H. Hartman, were more interested in the problematic relation of poets to their predecessors and to their own language. Bloom was especially concerned with the influence of Ralph Waldo Emerson on modern American poets. After developing a Freudian theory of literary influence in *The Anxiety of Influence* (1973) and *A Map of Misreading* (1975), Bloom reached a wide audience with *The Western Canon* (1994) and *Shakespeare: The Invention of the Human* (1998), both of which explored and defended the Western literary tradition.

Philosophers Richard Rorty and Stanley Cavell and critic Richard Poirier found a native parallel to European theory in the philosophy of Emerson and the writings of pragmatists such as William James and John Dewey. Emulating Dewey and Irving Howe, Rorty emerged as a social critic in *Achieving Our Country* (1998) and *Philosophy and Social Hope* (1999). Other academic critics also took a more political turn. Stephen Greenblatt's work on Shakespeare and other Elizabethan writers and Edward Said's essays in *The World, the Text, and the Critic* (1983) were influential in reviving historical approaches to literature that had long been neglected. Said's *Orientalism* (1978) and *Culture and Imperialism* (1993) directed attention to the effects of colonialism on the arts and society. His essays were collected in *Reflections on Exile* (2000). Other critics deflected this historical approach into the field of cultural studies, which erased the lines between "high" (elite) and "low" (popular) culture and often subsumed discussion of the arts to questions of ideology. Meanwhile, a wide range of feminist critics, beginning with Kate Millett, Ellen Moers, Sandra Gilbert, Susan Gubar, and Elaine Showalter, gave direction to new gender-based approaches to past and present writers. Critics who came to be known as queer theorists, such as Eve Kosofsky Sedgwick, produced innovative work on texts dealing with homosexuality, both overt and implicit.

All these methods yielded new dimensions of critical understanding, but in less adept hands they became so riddled with jargon or so intensely political and ideological that they lost touch with the general reader, with common sense itself, and with any tradition of accessible criticism. This drew criticism from a conservative perspective, as in Allan Bloom's *The Closing of the American Mind* (1987), and from writers on the left, such as Russell Jacoby in *The Last Intellectuals* (1987) and *Dogmatic Wisdom* (1994). Reactions against theory-based criticism set in during the 1990s not only with attacks on "political correctness" but also with a return to more informal and essayistic forms of criticism that emphasized the role of

Deconstruction

Deconstruction is a form of philosophical and literary analysis, derived mainly from work begun in the 1960s by the French philosopher Jacques Derrida, that questions the fundamental conceptual distinctions, or "oppositions," in Western philosophy through a close examination of the language and logic of philosophical and literary texts. In the 1970s the term was applied to work by Derrida, Paul de Man, J. Hillis Miller, and Barbara Johnson, among other scholars. In the 1980s it designated more loosely a range of radical theoretical enterprises in diverse areas of the humanities and social sciences, including— in addition to philosophy and literature—law, psychoanalysis, architecture, anthropology, theology, feminism, gay and lesbian studies, political theory, historiography, and film theory. In polemical discussions about intellectual trends of the late 20th century, deconstruction was sometimes used pejoratively to suggest nihilism and frivolous skepticism. In popular usage the term has come to mean a critical dismantling of tradition and traditional modes of thought.

Deconstruction's reception was coloured by its intellectual predecessors, most notably structuralism and New Criticism. Beginning in France in the 1950s, the structuralist movement in anthropology analyzed various cultural phenomena as general systems of "signs" and attempted to develop "metalanguages" of terms and concepts in which the different sign systems could be described. Structuralist methods were soon applied to other areas of the social sciences and humanities, including literary studies. Deconstruction offered a powerful critique of the possibility of creating detached, scientific metalanguages and was thus categorized (along with kindred efforts) as "post-structuralist." Anglo-American New Criticism sought to understand verbal works of art (especially poetry) as complex constructions made up of different and contrasting levels of literal and nonliteral meanings, and it emphasized the role of paradox and irony in these artifacts. Deconstructive readings, in contrast, treated works of art not as the harmonious fusion of literal and figurative meanings but as instances of the intractable conflicts between meanings of different types. They generally examined the individual work not as a self-contained artifact but as a product of relations with other texts or discourses, literary and nonliterary. Finally, these readings placed special emphasis on the ways in which the works themselves offered implicit critiques of the categories that critics used to analyze them. In the United States in the 1970s and '80s, deconstruction played a major role in the animation and transformation of literary studies by literary theory (often referred to simply as "theory"), which was concerned with questions about the nature of language, the production of meaning, and the relationship between literature and the numerous discourses that structure human experience and its histories.

the public intellectual and the need to reach a wider general audience. There was a revival of interest in literary journalism. Both older critics, such as Frank Lentricchia in *The Edge of Night* (1994) and Said in *Out of Place* (1999), and younger critics, including Alice Kaplan in *French Lessons* (1993), turned toward autobiography as a way of situating their own intellectual outlook and infusing personal expression into their work.

NOTEWORTHY POSTWAR CRITICS AND THEORISTS

Literary theory flourished in the period following World War II. From the canon-preserving work of Harold Bloom to the deconstruction of Paul de Man, notable critics and theorists who were working in the United States approached the study of literature and culture from a number of widely varying perspectives.

ALLAN BLOOM
(b. Sept. 14, 1930, Indianapolis, Ind..—d. Oct. 7, 1992, Chicago, Ill.)

Philosopher and writer Allan Bloom is best remembered for his provocative bestseller *The Closing of the American Mind: How Higher Education Has Failed Democracy and Impoverished the Souls of Today's Students* (1987). He was also known for his scholarly volumes of interpretive essays and translations of works by Jean-Jacques Rousseau and Plato.

Bloom received a Ph.D. in 1955 from the University of Chicago, where, under the tutelage of the German-born political philosopher Leo Strauss, he became a devotee of the Western classics and a proponent of the philosophical tenet of "transcultural truth." He taught at the University of Chicago (1955–60) and Yale (1962–63) and Cornell (1963–70) universities and was on the faculties of several foreign universities. He published such well-received works as *Shakespeare's Politics* (1964), a collection of essays, and a translation of Plato's *Republic* (1968).

In 1969 a group of students took control of Cornell's administration building and demanded that certain mandatory classes be dropped in favour of those deemed more "relevant" to them. After the university yielded to their demands, Bloom tendered his resignation, and in 1979 he returned to the University of Chicago. In *The Closing of the American Mind*, Bloom argued that universities no longer taught students how to think and that students, especially those attending the top schools, were unconcerned about the lessons of the past or about examining ideas in a historical context. His blistering critique, which offered no solutions to the crisis in education, blamed misguided curricula, rock music, television, and academic elitism for the spiritual impoverishment of students. A later collection of essays, *Giants and Dwarfs*, was published in 1990. Bloom's

Love and Friendship (1993) and *Shakespeare on Love and Friendship* (2000) appeared posthumously.

HAROLD BLOOM
(b. July 11, 1930, New York, N.Y.)

Literary critic Harold Bloom is known for his innovative interpretations of literary history and of the creation of literature.

Bloom's first language was Yiddish, and he also learned Hebrew before English. He attended Cornell (B.A., 1951)

Pioneering critic Harold Bloom is best known for his examinations of literary creation and interpretation, but he also had a passion for poetry and literature. Mark Mainz/Getty Images

and Yale (Ph.D., 1955) universities and began teaching at Yale in 1955. He also taught at New York University from 1988 to 2004. As a young man, he was much influenced by Northrop Frye's *Fearful Symmetry* (1947), a study of William Blake, and he later stated that he considered Frye "certainly the largest and most crucial literary critic in the English language" since Walter Pater and Oscar Wilde. Bloom's own early books, *Shelley's Mythmaking* (1959), *The Visionary Company: A Reading of English Romantic Poetry* (1961; rev. and enlarged ed. 1971), and *The Ringers in the Tower: Studies in Romantic Tradition* (1971), were creative studies of the Romantic poets and their work, then out of fashion. He examined the Romantic tradition from its beginnings in the 18th century to its influence on such late 20th-century poets as A.R. Ammons and Allen Ginsberg, quickly making a name for himself with his individual and challenging views.

With the publication of *Yeats* (1970), Bloom began to extend his critical theory, and in *The Anxiety of Influence* (1973) and *A Map of Misreading* (1975), he systematized one of his most original theories: that poetry results from poets deliberately misreading the works that influence them. *Figures of Capable Imagination* (1976) and several other works of the next decade develop and illustrate this theme.

One of Bloom's most controversial popular works appeared in his commentary on *The Book of J* (1990), published with David Rosenberg's translations of selected sections of the Pentateuch. In it, Bloom speculated that the earliest known texts of the Bible were written by a woman who lived during the time of David and Solomon and that the texts are literary rather than religious ones, on which later rewriters imposed beliefs of patriarchal Judaism. This work was one of a number of his books— including *Kabbalah and Criticism* (1975), *The American*

Religions (1992), *Omens of Millennium* (1996), *Jesus and Yahweh: The Names Divine* (2005), and the novel *The Flight to Lucifer* (1979) — to deal with religious subjects.

Perhaps Bloom's greatest legacy is his passion for poetry and literature of other types too. This is reflected in his best-known work, *The Western Canon: The Books and School of the Ages* (1994), which rejects the multiculturalism prevalent in late 20th-century academia. He once said of multiculturalism that "it means fifth-rate work by people full of resentment." In an interview published in 1995, Bloom reflected on the great authors of the Western world:

> *We have to read Shakespeare, and we have to study Shakespeare. We have to study Dante. We have to read Chaucer. We have to read Cervantes. We have to read the Bible, at least the King James Bible. We have to read certain authors....They provide an intellectual, I dare say, a spiritual value which has nothing to do with organized religion or the history of institutional belief. They remind us in every sense of re-minding us. They not only tell us things that we have forgotten, but they tell us things we couldn't possibly know without them, and they reform our minds. They make our minds stronger. They make us more vital.*

Bloom continued to both praise and analyze the literary canon in such books as *Shakespeare: The Invention of the Human* (1998), *How to Read and Why* (2000), and *Hamlet: Poem Unlimited* (2003). In addition, he selected the content of, and provided commentary for, the collection *The Best Poems of the English Language: From Chaucer Through Robert Frost* (2004).

In the mid-1980s Bloom began to work with Chelsea House Publishers to "chronicle all of Western literature." By 2005 he had edited more than 600 volumes. Series titles include Bloom's BioCritiques on individual authors, presented in a format that includes an extensive biography and critical analyses; Bloom's Guides, on individual literary masterpieces; Bloom's Literary Places, guides to such cities as London, Dublin, and Paris; Bloom's Major Literary Characters; Bloom's Modern Critical Interpretations, on major works; Bloom's Modern Critical Views, on major writers; and Bloom's Period Studies.

PAUL DE MAN

(b. Dec. 6, 1919, Antwerp, Belg.—d. Dec. 21, 1983, New Haven, Conn.)

Paul de Man was a Belgian-born literary critic and one of the major proponents of the critical theory known as deconstruction.

After graduating from the University of Brussels in 1942, de Man worked as a writer and translator until 1947, when he immigrated to the United States. After obtaining his Ph.D. at Harvard University, he taught at Harvard, Cornell, and Johns Hopkins. In 1970 he joined the faculty at Yale University, where he remained until his death.

At Yale, de Man wrote his groundbreaking book *Blindness and Insight: Essays in the Rhetoric of Contemporary Criticism* (1971), which argued that post-Kantian philosophy and literary criticism suffer from the tendency to confuse the structure of language with the principles that organize natural reality. With the publication of this work, Yale became the centre for deconstructive literary criticism in the United States. De Man's later works include *Allegories of Reading: Figural Language in Rousseau, Nietzsche, Rilke, and Proust* (1979), *The Rhetoric of Romanticism* (1984), and, on deconstruction, *The Resistance to Theory* (1986; written with Harold Bloom, Jacques Derrida, Geoffrey Hartman, and J. Hillis Miller) and *Aesthetic Ideology* (1988).

De Man's involvement from 1940 to 1942 with *Le Soir*, a Belgian pro-Nazi newspaper, was revealed in the late 1980s. His writings for the newspaper, including one overtly anti-Semitic essay, were collected and published under the title *Wartime Journalism, 1939–1943* (1988).

STANLEY FISH
(b. April 19, 1938, Providence, R.I.)

Literary critic Stanley Eugene Fish is particularly associated with reader-response criticism, according to which the meaning of a text is created, rather than discovered, by the reader; with neopragmatism, where critical practice is advanced over theory; and with the interpretive relationships between literature and law.

Fish was educated at the University of Pennsylvania (B.A., 1959) and Yale University (M.A., 1960; Ph.D., 1962). He taught at the University of California, Berkeley, Johns Hopkins University, Duke University, the University of Illinois at Chicago, and Florida International University in Miami.

In *Surprised by Sin: The Reader in "Paradise Lost"* (1967), Fish suggested that the subject of John Milton's masterpiece is in fact the reader, who is forced to undergo spiritual self-examination when led by Milton down the path taken by Adam, Eve, and Satan. In *Is There a Text in This Class?: The Authority of Interpretive Communities* (1980), Fish further developed his reader-as-subject theory. The essays in *Doing What Comes Naturally: Change, Rhetoric, and the Practice of Theory in Literary and Legal Studies* (1989) discuss a number of aspects of literary theory. Fish's subsequent works include *There's No Such Thing As Free Speech, and It's a Good Thing, Too* (1994), *Professional Correctness: Literary Studies and Political Change* (1995), *The Trouble with Principle* (1999), and *How Milton Works* (2001).

HENRY LOUIS GATES, JR.

(b. Sept. 16, 1950, Keyser, W.Va.)

Literary critic and scholar Henry Louis Gates, Jr., is known for his pioneering theories of African literature and African American literature. He introduced the notion of "signifyin'" to represent African and African American literary and musical history as a continuing reflection and reinterpretation of what has come before.

Henry Louis Gates, Jr., made great strides in the reading of African and African American literature with his concept of "signifyin'." HBO via Getty Images

Gates's father, Henry Louis Gates, Sr., worked in a paper mill and moonlighted as a janitor. His mother, Pauline Coleman Gates, cleaned houses. Gates graduated as valedictorian of his high school class in 1968 and attended a local junior college before enrolling at Yale University, where he received a bachelor's degree in history in 1973. After receiving two fellowships in 1970, he took a leave of absence from Yale to visit Africa, working as an anesthetist in a hospital in Tanzania and then traveling through other African nations. In 1973 he entered Clare College at the University of Cambridge, where one of his tutors was the Nigerian writer Wole Soyinka. Soyinka persuaded Gates to study literature instead of history and taught him much about the culture of the Yoruba, one of the largest Nigerian ethnic groups. After receiving his doctoral degree in English language and literature in 1979, Gates taught literature and African American studies at Yale University, Cornell University, Duke University, and Harvard University, where he was appointed W.E.B. DuBois Professor of the Humanities in 1991.

In 1980 Gates became codirector of the Black Periodical Literature Project at Yale. In the years that followed he earned a reputation as a "literary archaeologist" by recovering and collecting thousands of lost literary works (short stories, poems, reviews, and notices) by African American authors dating from the early 19th to the mid-20th century. In the early 1980s Gates rediscovered the earliest novel by an African American, Harriet E. Wilson's *Our Nig* (1859), by proving that the work was in fact written by an African American woman and not, as had been widely assumed, by a white man from the North. From the 1980s Gates edited many critical anthologies of African American literature, including *Black Literature and*

Literary Theory (1984), *Bearing Witness: Selections from African American Autobiography in the Twentieth Century* (1991), and (with Nellie Y. McKay) *The Norton Anthology of African American Literature* (1997).

Gates developed the notion of "signifyin'" in *Figures in Black: Words, Signs, and the "Racial" Self* (1987) and *The Signifying Monkey: A Theory of Afro-American Literary Criticism* (1988). Signifyin' is the practice of representing an idea indirectly, through a commentary that is often humourous, boastful, insulting, or provocative. Gates argued that the pervasiveness and centrality of signifyin' in African and African American literature and music means that all such expression is essentially a kind of dialogue with the literature and music of the past. Gates traced the practice of signifyin' to Esu, the trickster figure of Yoruba mythology, and to the figure of the "signifying monkey," with which Esu is closely associated. He applied the notion to the interpretation of slave narratives and showed how it informs the works of Phillis Wheatley, Zora Neale Hurston, Frederick Douglass, the early African American writers of periodical fiction, Ralph Ellison, Ishmael Reed, Alice Walker, and Wole Soyinka.

In *Loose Canons: Notes on the Culture Wars* (1992) and elsewhere Gates argued for the inclusion of African American literature in the Western canon. Other works by Gates include *Speaking of Race, Speaking of Sex: Hate Speech, Civil Rights, and Civil Liberties* (1994), *Colored People: A Memoir* (1994), *The Future of the Race* (1996; with Cornel West), *Thirteen Ways of Looking at a Black Man* (1997), *The Trials of Phillis Wheatley: America's First Black Poet and Her Encounters with the Founding Fathers* (2003), *America Behind the Color Line: Dialogues with African Americans* (2004), and *In Search of Our Roots* (2009).

BELL HOOKS
(b. Sept. 25, 1952, Hopkinsville, Ky.)

Scholar bell hooks is known for her work that examined the varied perceptions of black women and black women writers and the development of feminist identities.

Gloria Watkins grew up in a segregated community of the American South. At age 19 she began writing what would become her first full-length book, *Ain't I a Woman: Black Women and Feminism*, which was published in 1981. She studied English literature at Stanford University (B.A., 1973), the University of Wisconsin (M.A., 1976), and the University of California, Santa Cruz (Ph.D., 1983).

Hooks assumed her pseudonym, the name of her great-grandmother, to honour female legacies, preferring to spell it in all lowercase letters to focus attention on her message rather than herself. She taught English and ethnic studies at the University of Southern California from the mid-1970s, African and Afro-American studies at Yale University during the '80s, women's studies at Oberlin College, and English at the City College of New York during the 1990s and early 2000s. In 2004 she became a professor-in-residence at Berea College in Berea, Ky.

In the 1980s hooks established a support group for black women called the Sisters of the Yam, which she later used as the title of a book, published in 1993, celebrating black sisterhood. Her other writings include *Feminist Theory from Margin to Center* (1984), *Talking Back: Thinking Feminist, Thinking Black* (1989), *Black Looks: Race and Representation* (1992), *Killing Rage: Ending Racism* (1995), *Reel to Real: Race, Sex, and Class at the Movies* (1996), *Remembered Rapture: The Writer at Work* (1999), *Where We Stand: Class Matters* (2000), *Communion: The Female Search for Love* (2002), and the companion books *We Real Cool: Black Men and Masculinity* (2003) and *The Will to Change:*

Men, Masculinity, and Love (2004). She also wrote a number of autobiographical works, such as *Bone Black: Memories of Girlhood* (1996) and *Wounds of Passion: A Writing Life* (1997).

ALFRED KAZIN
(b. June 5, 1915, Brooklyn, N.Y.—d. June 5, 1998, New York, N.Y.)

Critic and author Alfred Kazin is noted for his studies of American literature and his autobiographical writings.

The son of Russian Jewish immigrants, Kazin attended the City College of New York during the Great Depression and then worked as a freelance book reviewer for the *New Republic* and other periodicals. At age 27 he wrote a sweeping historical study of modern American literature, *On Native Grounds* (1942), that won him instant recognition as a perceptive critic with a distinct point of view. The book traces the social and political movements that inspired successive stages of literary development in America from the time of William Dean Howells to that of William Faulkner.

Kazin's critical viewpoint and liberal political sensibilities were inextricably intertwined. He eschewed close textual or formal analysis, preferring instead to comprehend writers and their works in relation to the larger society and times in which they lived. In a sequel to his first book, *Bright Book of Life* (1973), he surveyed American literature from the writings of Ernest Hemingway to those of Norman Mailer. Among Kazin's other studies of American literature are the essay collections *The Inmost Leaf* (1955) and *Contemporaries* (1962); another broad survey of American prose, *An American Procession* (1984); and *God and the American Writer* (1997). He also published book-length studies of F. Scott Fitzgerald and Theodore Dreiser, edited anthologies of the works of Ralph Waldo Emerson and Nathaniel Hawthorne, and was a visiting professor at various universities.

Kazin's sketches of literary personalities reveal much about both writers and their eras. He wrote three autobiographical works: *A Walker in the City* (1951), which lyrically evokes his youth in the Brownsville section of Brooklyn, *Starting Out in the Thirties* (1965), memoirs of his young manhood, and *New York Jew* (1978), about his life during the years from World War II to the 1970s.

J. HILLIS MILLER
(b. March 5, 1928, Newport News, Va.)

Literary critic J. Hillis Miller was initially associated with the Geneva group of critics and, later, with the Yale school and deconstruction. Miller was important in connecting North American criticism with Continental philosophical thought.

Joseph Hillis Miller graduated from Oberlin College in 1948 and received an M.A. and Ph.D. from Harvard University in 1949 and 1952, respectively. After teaching English at Williams College for one year, he held positions at Johns Hopkins University (1953–72), Yale University (1972–86), and the University of California, Irvine (from 1986). Miller was president of the Modern Language Association of America in 1986 and contributed significantly to professional academic institutions and organizations throughout his career.

Like the Geneva group of critics, Miller argued that literature is a tool for understanding the mind of the writer. His criticism emphasized theological concerns, as in *Poets of Reality: Six Twentieth-Century Writers* (1965), *The Form of Victorian Fiction: Thackeray, Dickens, Trollope, George Eliot, Meredith, and Hardy* (1968), and *The Disappearance of God: Five Nineteenth-Century Writers* (1963). He drew heavily on ideas of the absence or death of the divine. By 1970, however, he had joined the deconstructionist critics at Yale, where he often defended deconstuction against charges of nihilism. Although Miller's literary scholarship was always concerned with language and particularly with figuration and rhetoric, his later work stresses these topics with a newly attuned attention to their relevance for theory. Evidence of this concern with the mutual inter-penetration of literature and literary theory can be seen in *Fiction and Repetition* (1982), *The Linguistic Moment* (1985), *The Ethics of Reading: Kant, de Man, Eliot, Trollope, James, and Benjamin* (1987), *Versions of Pygmalion* (1990), *Victorian Subjects* (1991), *Hawthorne and History: Defacing It* (1991), *Topographies* (1995), *Reading Narrative* (1998), *Speech Acts in Literature* (2001), and *On Literature* (2002).

KATE MILLETT
(b. Sept. 14, 1934, St. Paul, Minn.)

Feminist, author, and artist Kate Millett was an early and influential figure in the women's liberation movement, whose first book, *Sexual Politics*, began her exploration of the dynamics of power in relation to gender and sexuality.

Millett earned a bachelor's degree with honours in 1956 from the University of Minnesota, where she was also elected to Phi Beta Kappa. Two years later she was awarded a master's degree with first-class honours from the University of Oxford. After teaching English briefly at the University of North Carolina at Greensboro, Millett moved to New York City to pursue a career as an artist. To support herself she taught kindergarten in Harlem. In 1961 she moved to Tokyo, where she taught English at Waseda University and also studied sculpting. By the time she married Japanese sculptor Fumio Yoshimura in 1965, however, Millett was back in New York City, teaching

English and philosophy at Barnard College. (The couple divorced in 1985.) At the same time, she pursued a doctorate at Columbia University, and in 1970 she was awarded a Ph.D. with distinction. Her thesis, a work combining literary analysis with sociology and anthropology, was published that same year as *Sexual Politics*. The book, which defined the goals and strategies of the feminist movement, was an overnight success, transforming Millett into a public figure.

The celebrity came at a personal cost, as Millett revealed in a 1974 autobiographical work, *Flying*, which explains the torment she suffered as a result of her views in general and of her disclosure that she was a lesbian in particular. She wrote two more autobiographical books, *Sita* (1977) and *A.D.: A Memoir* (1995). *The Basement* (1979) is a factual account of a young woman's abuse, torture, and murder at the hands of a group of teenagers led by an older woman who had been appointed her protector. Millett's subsequent books dealt with the political oppression in Iran after the rise of Ayatollah Ruhollah Khomeini (*Going to Iran*, 1982), with her own personal experiences as a psychiatric patient (*The Loony Bin Trip*, 1990), with the issue of cruelty in general (*The Politics of Cruelty*, 1994), and with the problems of aging, as seen through the struggles of her mother (*Mother Millett*, 2001).

EDWARD SAID

(b. Nov. 1, 1935, Jerusalem—d. Sept. 25, 2003, New York, N.Y.)

Edward Said was a Palestinian American academic, political activist, and literary critic who examined literature in light of social and cultural politics and was an outspoken proponent of the political rights of the Palestinian people and the creation of an independent Palestinian state. In addition to his political and academic pursuits, Said was an accomplished musician and pianist.

Said's father, Wadie (William) Ibrahim, was a wealthy businessman who had lived some time in the United States and apparently, at some point, took U.S. citizenship. In 1947 Wadie moved the family from Jerusalem to Cairo to avoid the conflict that was beginning over the United Nations partition of Palestine into separate Jewish and Arab areas. In Cairo Said was educated in English-language schools before transferring to the exclusive Northfield

Much of literary critic Edward Said's work sharply reflects his personal beliefs. Said wrote numerous books concerning the Arab world and the political rights of Palestinians. Jean-Christian Bourcart/Getty Images

Mount Hermon School in Massachusetts in the United States in 1951. He attended Princeton University (B.A., 1957) and Harvard University (M.A., 1960; Ph.D., 1964), where he specialized in English literature. He joined the faculty of Columbia University as a lecturer in English in 1963 and in 1967 was promoted to assistant professor of English and comparative literature. His first book, *Joseph Conrad and the Fiction of Autobiography* (1966), was an expansion of his doctoral thesis. The book examines Conrad's short stories and letters for the underlying tension of the author's narrative style and is concerned with the cultural dynamics of beginning a work of literature or scholarship.

Said was promoted to full professor in 1969, received his first of several endowed chairs in 1977, and in 1978 published *Orientalism*, his best-known work and one of the most influential scholarly books of the 20th century. In it Said examines Western scholarship of the "Orient," specifically of the Arab Islamic world (although he was an Arab Christian), and argues that early scholarship by Westerners in that region was biased and projected a false and stereotyped vision of "otherness" on the Islamic world that facilitated and supported Western colonial policy.

Although he never taught any courses on the Middle East, Said wrote numerous books and articles in his support of Arab causes and Palestinian rights. He was especially critical of U.S. and Israeli policy in the region, and this led him into numerous, often bitter, polemics with supporters of those two countries. He was elected to the Palestine National Council (the Palestinian legislature in exile) in 1977. Although he supported a peaceful resolution of the Israeli-Palestinian conflict, he became highly critical of the Oslo peace process between the Palestine Liberation Organization and Israel in the early 1990s.

His books about the Middle East include *The Question of Palestine* (1979), *Covering Islam: How the Media and the Experts Determine How We See the Rest of the World* (1981), *Blaming the Victims: Spurious Scholarship and the Palestinian Question* (1988; coedited with Christopher Hitchens), *The Politics of Dispossession* (1994), and *Peace and Its Discontents: Essays on Palestine in the Middle East Peace Process* (1995). Among his other notable books are *The World, the Text, and the Critic* (1983), *Nationalism, Colonialism, and Literature: Yeats and Decolonization* (1988), *Musical Elaborations* (1991), and *Culture and Imperialism* (1993). His autobiography, *Out of Place* (1999), reflects the ambivalence he felt over living in both the Western and Eastern traditions.

ELAINE SHOWALTER

(b. Jan. 21, 1941, Boston, Mass.)

Literary critic and teacher Elaine Showalter is the founder of gynocritics, a school of feminist criticism concerned with "woman as writer...with the history, themes, genres, and structures of literature by women."

Showalter studied English at Bryn Mawr College (B.A., 1962), Brandeis University (M.A., 1964), and the University of California, Davis (Ph.D., 1970). She joined the faculty of Douglass College, the women's division of Rutgers University, in 1969, where she developed women's studies courses and began editing and contributing articles to books and periodicals about women's literature. She later taught at Rutgers and Princeton University, neither of which hired women when she began her teaching career. She retired from Princeton as professor emeritus in 2003. Showalter also spent time as a freelance journalist and media commentator.

Showalter developed her doctoral thesis into her first book, *A Literature of Their Own: British Women Novelists from Brontë to Lessing* (1977), a pioneering study in which she created a critical framework for analyzing literature by women. Her next book, *The Female Malady: Women, Madness, and English Culture, 1830–1980* (1985), was a historical examination of women and the practice of psychiatry. She also wrote *Sexual Anarchy: Gender and Culture at the Fin de Siècle* (1990); *Sister's Choice: Tradition and Change in American Women's Writing* (1991); *Hystories: Historical Epidemics and Modern Culture* (1997), a controversial exploration of the history of mass hysteria; *Inventing Herself: Claiming a Feminist Intellectual Heritage* (2001), which follows the evolution of the feminist intellectual from the 18th to the 21st century; *Teaching Literature* (2003); *Faculty Towers: The Academic Novel and Its Discontents* (2005), an analysis of the academic novel and its relation to real-world institutes of higher education; and *A Jury of Her Peers* (2009), a survey of women's writing in the United States from its origins through the 1990s. Showalter edited several volumes, including *The New Feminist Criticism* (1985) and *Daughters of Decadence: Women Writers of the Fin de Siècle* (1993).

LIONEL TRILLING
(b. July 4, 1905, New York, N.Y. — d. Nov. 5, 1975, New York)

Lionel Trilling was a literary critic and teacher whose criticism was informed by psychological, sociological, and philosophical methods and insights.

Educated at Columbia University (M.A., 1926; Ph.D., 1938), Trilling taught briefly at the University of Wisconsin and at Hunter College in New York City. In 1931 he joined the faculty of Columbia, where he remained for the rest of his life. Trilling was married to Diana Trilling, née Rubin, also a critic and writer.

Trilling's critical writings include studies of Matthew Arnold (1939) and E.M. Forster (1943), as well as collections of literary essays: *The Liberal Imagination* (1950), *Beyond Culture: Essays on Literature and Learning* (1965), and *Sincerity and Authenticity* and *Mind in the Modern World* (both 1972). He also wrote *Freud and the Crisis of Our Culture* (1955) and *The Life and Work of Sigmund Freud* (1962). Although Trilling maintained an interest in Freud and psychoanalysis throughout his intellectual career, his criticism was not based on any one system of thought. He saw his role and the role of all useful criticism as similar to that of his important predecessor Matthew Arnold: the "disinterested endeavour to learn and propagate the best that is known and thought in the world." To do so, Trilling brought a wide range of ideas and positions to bear on his subjects. He covered many social and cultural topics, but Trilling remained concerned with the tradition of humanistic thought and with the goal of educating and stimulating the enlightened middle classes.

Trilling's novel *The Middle of the Journey* (1947) concerns the moral and political developments of the liberal mind in America in the 1930s and '40s. In 2008 a second novel, discovered and edited by scholar Geraldine Murphy, was published posthumously. Titled *The Journey Abandoned*, it follows the attempts of a graspingly ambitious young critic to make his name writing the biography of a reclusive writer turned physicist.

GORE VIDAL

(b. Oct. 3, 1925, West Point, N.Y.)

The prolific novelist, playwright, and essayist Gore Vidal is noted for his irreverent and intellectually adroit novels

The outspoken and often irreverent author and critic Gore Vidal was extolled for his wit. Charles Gallay/Getty Images

and his numerous essays that cover a wide range of topics, both literary and nonliterary.

While a student at Philips Exeter Academy in New Hampshire, Eugene Luther Vidal changed his first name to "Gore," his mother's maiden name. He graduated from Exeter in 1943 and served in the U.S. Army in World War II. Thereafter, he resided in many parts of the world—the east and west coasts of the United States, Europe, North Africa, and Central America. His first novel, *Williwaw* (1946), which was based on his wartime experiences, was praised by the critics, and his third novel, *The City and the Pillar* (1948), shocked the public with its direct and unadorned examination of a homosexual main character. Vidal's next five novels, including *Messiah* (1954), were received coolly by critics and were commercial failures. Abandoning novels, he turned to writing plays for the stage, television, and motion pictures and was successful in all three media. His best-known dramatic works from the next decade were *Visit to a Small Planet* (produced for television, 1955; on Broadway, 1957; for film, 1960) and *The Best Man* (play 1960; film 1964).

Vidal returned to writing novels with *Julian* (1964), a sympathetic fictional portrait of Julian the Apostate, the 4th-century pagan Roman emperor who opposed Christianity. *Washington, D.C.* (1967), an ironic examination of political morality in the U.S. capital, was the first of a series of several popular novels known as the Narratives of Empire, which vividly re-created prominent figures and events in American history—*Burr* (1974), *1876* (1976), *Lincoln* (1984), *Empire* (1987), *Hollywood* (1990), and *The Golden Age* (2000). *Lincoln*, a compelling portrait of Pres. Abraham Lincoln's complex personality as viewed through the eyes of some of his closest associates during the American Civil War, is particularly notable. Another success was the comedy *Myra Breckinridge* (1968; film

1970), in which Vidal lampooned both transsexuality and contemporary American culture. In *Rocking the Boat* (1962), *Reflections upon a Sinking Ship* (1969), *The Second American Revolution* (1982), *United States: Essays, 1952–1992* (1993; National Book Award), *Imperial America: Reflections of the United States of Amnesia* (2004), and other essay collections, he incisively analyzed contemporary American politics and government. He also wrote two autobiographies: *Palimpsest: A Memoir* (1995) and *Point to Point Navigation: A Memoir, 1964 to 2006* (2006). Vidal was noted for his outspoken political opinions and for the witty and satirical observations he was wont to make as a guest on talk shows.

CORNEL WEST
(b. June 2, 1953, Tulsa, Oklahoma)

A philosopher, scholar of African American studies, and political activist, Cornel West wrote the influential book *Race Matters* (1993). In the book West lamented what he saw as the spiritual impoverishment of the African American underclass and critically examined the "crisis of black leadership" in the United States.

West's father was a civilian U.S. Air Force administrator and his mother an elementary school teacher and eventually a principal. During West's childhood the family settled in an African American working-class neighbourhood in Sacramento, Calif. There West regularly attended services at the local Baptist church, where he listened to moving testimonials of privation, struggle, and faith from parishioners whose grandparents had been slaves. Another influence on West during this time was the Black Panther Party, whose Sacramento offices were near the church. The Panthers impressed upon him the importance of political activism at the local level and introduced him to the writings of Karl Marx.

In 1970, at age 17, West entered Harvard University on a scholarship. He graduated magna cum laude three years later with a bachelor's degree in Middle Eastern languages and literature. He attended graduate school in philosophy at Princeton University, where he was influenced by the American pragmatist philosopher Richard Rorty. (West briefly abandoned work on his dissertation to write a novel, which was never published.) After receiving his doctoral degree in 1980, West taught philosophy, religion, and African American studies at several colleges and universities, including Union Theological Seminary, Yale University (including the Yale Divinity School), the University of Paris, Princeton University, and Harvard University, where he was appointed Alphonse Fletcher, Jr., University Professor in 1998. He returned to Princeton in 2002.

West's work was characteristically wide-ranging, eclectic, original, and provocative. His several books analyzing issues of race, class, and justice or tracing the history of philosophy typically combined a political perspective based on democratic socialism, a Christian moral sensibility, and a philosophical orientation informed by the tradition of American pragmatism. His best-known work, *Race Matters*, a collection of essays, was published exactly one year after the start of riots in Los Angeles that were sparked by the acquittal of four white policemen on charges of aggravated assault in the beating of Rodney King, an African American motorist. The book discussed the pervasive despair and "nihilism" of African Americans in poverty and criticized African American leaders for pursuing strategies that West believed were shortsighted, narrow-minded, or self-serving. West also considered issues such as black-Jewish relations, the renewed popularity of Malcolm X, and the significance of the Los Angeles riots themselves.

West was always a political activist as well as an academic, and he did not hesitate to participate in demonstrations or to lend his name or presence to causes he felt were just. At times his activism created tensions with the administrations of the universities where he taught. In 2001 the new Harvard University president, Laurence Summers, reportedly admonished West in private for devoting too much time to political activity and other extracurricular pursuits. Their dispute was soon joined by supporters and detractors of West both inside and outside the academy, who debated not only the merits of West's scholarship but also the commitment of Summers and Harvard to affirmative action programs. Eventually West resigned his position at Harvard and moved to Princeton.

West's other works include *The American Evasion of Philosophy: A Genealogy of Pragmatism* (1989), *The Ethical Dimensions of Marxist Thought* (1991), *Beyond Eurocentrism and Multiculturalism* (1993), and *Democracy Matters: Winning the Fight Against Imperialism* (2004). In 2001 he recorded a raplike spoken-word CD entitled *Sketches of My Culture*. In 2003 he appeared as the character Councillor West in the popular movies *The Matrix Reloaded* and *The Matrix Revolutions*.

EPILOGUE

American literature since the end of World War II has been notable for its vast diversity of texts. Where the works of the country's authors were once fairly homogeneous, the rise of postmodernism in the latter half of the 20th century led to writings that in form and substance did not resemble anything seen previously. As mass media became both more varied and increasingly pervasive, American authors began to interrogate this new public reality in novel ways. From the recursive, self-aware narratives of David Foster Wallace to Frank O'Hara's multimedia "poem-paintings," American literary works after 1945 are impossible to easily define. If the past half-century is any guide, one of the only sureties of the future of American literature is that the coming works of the 21st century will take new and unexpected forms. Nevertheless, whatever form it takes, the literature of the United States will continue to reflect and, in turn, shape the character of the country.

absurdists Writers who shared a belief that human life was essentially without meaning or purpose and that valid communication was impossible. They deemed the human condition as having deteriorated to a state of absurdity.

allegory A symbolic fictional narrative that conveys a meaning not explicitly set forth in the narrative.

Beat movement A 1950s American social and literary movement whose members expressed feelings of alienation from conventional society by adopting the dress, manners, and vocabulary of jazz musicians.

bildungsroman A novel that deals with the moral and psychological growth of an individual. The term originates from German literature.

black humour A form of comedy that juxtaposes morbid or ghastly elements with comical ones underscoring the senselessness or futility of life.

Black Mountain poets A loosely associated group of poets that formed an important part of the avant-garde of American poetry in the 1950s.

catch-22 Refers to a condition that trips one up no matter which way one turns; coined in Joseph Heller's novel of the same name.

cyberpunk Science fiction that combines a cynical and tough, or "punk," sensibility with futuristic cybernetic technology.

cyberspace In science fiction, a computer-simulated reality that shows the nature of information. It foreshadowed virtual reality technology and was created by science fiction writer William Gibson.

deconstruction A form of literary analysis that questions the fundamental concepts of Western philosophy through a close examination of the language and logic of philosophical and literary texts.

deep image poets Poets, including Robert Bly, who sought spiritual intensity and transcendence of the self rather than confessional immediacy.

Freudian criticism Literary criticism that interprets works using Sigmund Freud's psychoanalytic theory. It takes into consideration the known psychological conflicts of its author or, conversely, attempts to construct the author's psychic life from unconscious revelations in his work.

Fugitives A group of poets with a shared a commitment to the South and its regional traditions; they published the influential literary magazine *The Fugitive* (1922–25).

gonzo journalism Highly personal, subjective, even eccentric, reporting created by Hunter S. Thompson.

gynocritics School of feminist criticism that focuses on women as writers, specifically their literary history, themes, and genres.

hard-boiled fiction A tough, unsentimental style of American crime writing containing graphic sex and violence; vivid but often sordid urban backgrounds; and fast-paced, slangy dialogue.

Kafkaesque Relating to or suggesting the writing of Franz Kafka, usually having a terrifyingly complex, strange, or irrational quality.

magic realism A chiefly Latin American narrative form of storytelling characterized by fantastic or mythical elements woven into seemingly realistic fiction.

metafiction Postmodern self-reflective fiction that questions the nature of representation, and often imitates or parodies previously written fiction rather than social reality.

modernism In the arts and literature, a radical break with the past and the concurrent search for new forms of expression. Modernism fostered a period of experimentation in literature and the arts from the late 19th to the mid-20th century, particularly in the years following World War I.

new journalism A genre combining the imaginative subjectivity of literature with the more objective qualities of journalism.

picaresque novel A genre of literature native to Spain usually featuring as its protagonist a rogue, essentially an antihero, living by his or her wits and concerned only with staying alive.

poetic diction Grandiose, elevated, and unfamiliar language often liberally laden with archaic terms and allegedly the prerogative of poetry.

signifyin' The practice of representing an idea indirectly through humourous, boastful, insulting, or provocative commentary; noted by Henry Louis Gates, Jr as a common technique in African and African American literature.

social realism A trend in American art forms, originating in the 1930s, that examined themes of social protest in a naturalistic or quasi-expressionist manner.

surrealism A movement in literature and the visual arts that encouraged the creation of works that defied reason but focused on positive expression.

BIBLIOGRAPHY

L iterary histories and major anthologies include Robert E. Spiller et al. (eds.), *Literary History of the United States*, 4th ed., rev., 2 vol. (1974), a standard general work; Marcus Cunliffe (ed.), *American Literature Since 1900*, new ed. (1987, reissued 1993); Walter Blair et al. (eds.), *The Literature of the United States*, 3rd ed., 2 vol. (1966); and Cleanth Brooks, R. W. B. Lewis, and Robert Penn Warren (compilers), *American Literature: The Makers and the Making*, 2 vol. (1973). Since the 1980s anthologies have shifted to a multicultural viewpoint with broad coverage of writing by women and minorities. The most controversial example has been Paul Lauter and Richard Yarborough (eds.), *The Heath Anthology of American Literature*, 2nd ed., 2 vol. (1994). Recent full-scale literary histories representing the work of younger scholars include Emory Elliott et al. (eds.), *The Columbia Literary History of the United States* (1991); and Sacvan Bercovitch and Cyrus R.K. Patell (eds.), *The Cambridge History of American Literature* (1994–2005). Blanche E. Gelfant (ed.), *The Columbia Companion to the Twentieth-Century American Short Story* (2000), is a comprehensive guide to short fiction.

Studies that focus on the period from the Civil War to the 20th century include the following: Arthur Hobson Quinn, *A History of the American Drama, from the Civil War to the Present Day,* rev. ed. (1964, reprinted 1980), the most thorough treatment; Alfred Kazin, *On Native Grounds: An Interpretation of Modern American Prose Literature* (1942, reprinted 1982), a brilliantly written critical history; and

Morton Dauwen Zabel (ed.), *Literary Opinion in America,* 3rd ed., rev., 2 vol. (1962).

Feminist criticism of American fiction can be found in Judith Fetterley, *The Resisting Reader* (1978). Radical and ethnic writing between the two world wars has been studied by Walter B. Rideout, *The Radical Novel in the United States, 1900–1954* (1956; reissued 1992) and Daniel Aaron, *Writers on the Left* (1961, reissued 1992). The long history of African American literature has been explored by Robert A. Bone, *The Negro Novel in America*, rev. ed. (1965); Robert B. Stepto, *From Behind the Veil*, 2nd ed. (1991); and Henry Louis Gates, Jr., *The Signifying Monkey* (1988). A succinct survey of Jewish American writing can be found in Allen Guttmann, *The Jewish Writer in America* (1971).

Critical studies of post–World War II fiction include Tony Tanner, *City of Words* (1971), valuable for understanding contemporary metafiction; Morris Dickstein, *Gates of Eden: American Culture in the Sixties* (1977, reprinted 1997), and *Leopards in the Temple* (2002), which place postwar writers in their cultural context; Frederick R. Karl, *American Fictions, 1940–1980* (1983), a comprehensive study; and Daniel Hoffman (ed.), *Harvard Guide to Contemporary American Writing* (1979), a collection of essays by major scholars. Studies of postwar poetry can be found in Charles Molesworth, *The Fierce Embrace* (1979); and Helen Vendler, *Part of Nature, Part of Us: Modern American Poets* (1980). Studies of modern American drama include Harold Clurman, *The Fervent Years* (1945, reprinted 1983), dealing with the 1930s; and C. W. E. Bigsby, *A Critical Introduction to Twentieth-Century American Drama,* 3 vol. (1982–85). Studies of 20th-century American critics can be found in Frank Lentricchia, *After the New Criticism* (1980); and Morris Dickstein, *Double Agent: The Critic and Society* (1992). American Literature

INDEX